Marxist Economics

A Popular Introduction to the
Three Volumes of Marx's "Das Kapital"

by Ernest Untermann

Red and Black Publishers, St Petersburg, Florida

First published as "Marxian Economics" by Charles Kerr Co., Chicago, 1907

Library of Congress Cataloging-in-Publication Data

Untermann, Ernest.
   Marxist economics : a popular introduction to the three volumes of Marx's "Das kapital" / by Ernest Untermann.
      p. cm.
   "First published as "Marxian Economics" by Charles Kerr Co., Chicago, 1907."
   ISBN 978-1-934941-71-3
1. Marx, Karl, 1818-1883. Kapital. 2. Marxian economics. 3. Socialism. I. Untermann, Ernest. Marxian economics. II. Title.
   HB501.M37U58 2009
   335.4'12--dc22

                                                        2009016084

Red and Black Publishers, PO Box 7542, St Petersburg, Florida, 33734
Contact us at: info@RedandBlackPublishers.com
   Printed and manufactured in the United States of America

Contents

Foreword

Since October, 1894, the complete economic theories of Karl Marx, as laid down by himself and his fellow worker Frederick Engels, in the three volumes of "Capital," have been before the teachers and students of all classes.

By that time, the contents of the first and second volumes of their work had been assimilated by hundreds of thousands. Especially volume I, which deals specifically with the relation between wage workers and capitalists, had long become "The Bible of the Working Class," at least of the class-conscious portion of this class. Volume I has now been translated into all the principal languages, not only of Europe, but of the world, and has become the standard textbook of economics for the vast majority of all revolutionary organizations of the proletariat.

This fact speaks convincingly for the soundness of the essential claims made by the Marxian theories. Nevertheless, when volume III appeared in Europe, the spokesmen of official political economy made the same blundering attempts to refute it which they had made with so little success in the case of volumes I and II. The only tangible result of these attacks has been to bring the Marxian theories to the attention of thousands who would not have been reached by the propagandists of the working class.

The best policy of the ruling classes in dealing with revolutionary literature has always been to kill it by silence. As soon as this policy is no longer practicable, every attempt to discredit the revolutionary theories by criticism becomes a means of making propaganda for them among circles that would otherwise remain in ignorance of them.

The Marxian theories derive their vitality out of the life of the working class itself. All the essential points of these theories are vindicated day by day through the experiences which the working class makes in its development under capitalist rule.

It is evident that theories so intimately reflecting the vital movements of the most essential class in modern society must spread in proportion as this class is pushed forward by historical development into the position which these theories foreshadow. A critique of its theories cannot stop such a movement any more than a critique of the Copernican theories could stop the Earth from revolving around the Sun.

But the professors of the ruling class have never been able to distinguish between a scheme and a historical process. They still flatter themselves that their learned proof for the unsoundness of Marxian economics will dissolve the socialist parties. And although every new election deepens the grave of their hopes, they are still busy rescuing from the pernicious influence of Marxian ideas a social system which lives only by undermining its own foundation.

The appearance of Volume III of Marx's "Capital" seems to have been the signal for a concerted action on the part of all capitalist universities against the economics of Socialism. Even the United States have received the blessings of this awakening civilization in the shape of translations of the works of Bohm-Bawerk, Sombart, Schiiflle, Le Bon, and others. In this way, the critiques of Marx's complete work have reached America before the work itself has been presented to American readers. For the great majority of American professors and students are not familiar with the German language and have no opportunity to study the work which some of those translations criticise so trenchantly.

The second volume of "Capital" was not published in the English language until July, 1907, and the third volume, although nearly completed in manuscript, will not be ready for publication before 1908.

It is very thoughtful of those learned critics of Marx to acquaint their pupils at least with criticisms of his theories, so long as these theories themselves cannot be studied in the original or in epitomes. To any one familiar with the "freedom of science" in universities controlled by the pocketbooks of American millionaires it is quite plain that this speedy introduction of works criticising (and above all misrepresenting) the Marxian theories was dictated by the most disinterested motives.

No doubt great masses of American teachers and students, who read these translated critiques, have become duly impressed with the importance of a work which requires an acquaintance with its critics even before the author himself is introduced.

Since so high an authority as President Roosevelt has emphatically declared that everyone is assured a "square deal" in this country, I have been haunted night and day by visions of American professors and students protesting strenuously against an unfair policy, which compels them to read a critique of a work without enabling them to judge of the merits of this work for themselves. It looks too much like paternalism of the patriarchal kind.

In order to put an end to this unworthy and embarrassing situation, I offer to American readers this popular synopsis of the complete Marxian economics, so that every one who is asked to read a critique of these theories may have an opportunity to see for himself what they really stand for.

Of course, I cannot deny that my little volume will very likely be read by a few thousand working people. Indeed, I think it will be read by more working people than professors and university students. But why should that give pause to anyone, so long as the belief prevails that capitalist professors and students can stop the growth of proletarian class-consciousness by distorting Marxian theories? Armed with the power which a diligent study of those critiques and of my little work will confer upon them, these professors and university students can go out among the working class and, by their superior intelligence, quickly undo all the harm caused by Marxian theories. I hope they will try it.

The third volume of "Capital" has been a veritable bugaboo for the economists of the ruling classes. When years passed without its appearance, it was hinted that this third volume did not exist at all but was only a subterfuge of Marx, by which he concealed his lack of scientific argument. Then, when it really did appear, it was claimed that it completely disavowed the theories laid down in Volumes I and II. And when some pupils of Marx demonstrated conclusively that the Marxian theory of value and surplus-value was carried consistently through all three volumes, the old claim was revived that these theories themselves were unsound. This last subterfuge derived additional strength from Eduard Bernstein's critique of Marxian theories. His critique, professedly undertaken in the interest and in defense of the Marxian theories, with a view to eliminating some alleged inconsistencies from them, served nevertheless as a weapon against Marxism, contrary to the intentions of Bernstein. Still, even so, all the professional efforts have redounded to the benefit of the proletarian revolution, and will do so in the future.

Marx followed a consistent plan in his three volumes. But this is not apparent on the surface. What makes the study of the original so tedious for the untrained student is this: Marx develops his theories step by step from the simplest cell of capitalist economy, a commodity, to the most complicated practical operations of capitalists under actual competition. We see the Marxian theories of value and surplus-value first in the making under assumed ideal conditions. Link by link we see them rising before our eyes. Occasionally we see some of these links compared with theories of some ancient or medieval or early capitalist economists. Then again the analysis pauses, in order to test or emphasize some point by illustrations from history. After that the analysis is spun further along to some other point, and so forth with variations. The illness and premature death of the author left the work in an unfinished condition. His comrade Engels completed it from notes left by the deceased. These circumstances give to the whole work the air of crude and unpolished roughness, so long as only its surface is touched. And more than that not one of the Marx critics has ever touched. But on closer scrutiny the logical consistency and organic interrelation of the three volumes becomes palpable. Volume I lays bare the secret mechanism of the sphere of production. Volume II discloses the mainsprings in the sphere of circulation. Volume III finally applies the results of the two preceding volumes to typical conditions of capitalist industry and commerce, showing the interrelation between production and circulation.

It is true that Marx modifies his theories in Volume III. But he does not abandon them. And he modifies them only to the extent that he carries his argument from the assumed ideal conditions of Volumes I and II nearer and nearer to the real conditions of capitalist industry and commerce. In the same way, a scientist would modify his argument when analyzing the law of gravity and passing from the ideal conditions of a vacuum pump to the complicated conditions in the open air, under which the law of gravity operates on the surface of the earth.

This analogy is often waved aside by our opponents with the assertion that the scientist experimenting on gravity does not abstract from any essential conditions of gravitation, while Marx, in abstracting from the actual conditions of capitalist production and circulation, eliminates all the essential elements which affect the value of commodities. Those who argue in this way abstract from all the essential elements of Marx's work and operate with an unessential abstraction of their own, which they label Marx's theory of value.

None of the existing popularizations of Marxian economics is a presentation of the complete theories of all three volumes. So far as Volumes II and III have received any attention in subsequent editions of popularizations of Volume I, it has been done in a disconnected way. No popularization has so far presented an organically complete outline of Marx's theories. Perhaps such an outline will yet be written by the man best equipped to do so, Karl Kautsky. There is decidedly a demand for such a popularization. The existing popularizations of Volume I have certainly filled a useful place in our literature. But they do not appeal equally to all classes of students, because they dwell almost exclusively upon the purely theoretical side of the question, and leave the historical side largely in the background.

It is the historical side which appeals most strongly to a large class of students. For this reason I have not attempted in this little volume to write a summary of the Marxian analyses in the theoretical order followed by Marx. I have rather endeavored to develop the entire subject historically. This enables me to enliven the subject and to appeal not only to the critical intellect, but also to the emotional side of the reader's reason. Yet this emotional style does not prevent me from adhering strictly to facts.

I follow no subjective standard of sentimental feeling, nor do I judge historical events and personalities by any such standard. Neither do I judge of events and personalities by the light of a supposed eternal standard of supernatural right and justice. My estimate of the ethical value of things or processes is rather based upon a genetic and historical foundation. Just as in the evolution of animals and plants we have built up a genetic table of organic development, which enables us to compare the various forms, qualities, species, etc., and tell at a glance, whether any one of them represents a forward or backward step in the general line of organic advance, in other words, whether any one form is evolutionary or reactionary from the point of view of the entire scale, so in the history of mankind I use the method of dialectic monism and historical materialism to compare the ideas, or customs, laws, etc., of different epochs and to ascertain to what extent they represent an evolution or a reaction in the general advance of mankind.

The impression prevails in many circles that the inductive and objective method of investigation, which is characteristic of historical materialism, forbids a sympathetic treatment of history. For my part, I do not see the logic of this assumption. It seems to me, rather, that at the bottom of it lies a confusion of ideas. Certainly there is plenty of genuine feeling in all of Marx's and Engels' work, and it does not militate in the least against the soundness of their analyses and conclusions. To inject human feeling into a scientific work is not the same as judging historical events and individuals by a sentimental standard of subjective feeling. The individualist historians of the bourgeoisie have brought discredit upon human feeling by degrading it to a sniveling standard of sentimentalism. On the other hand, feeling based upon an inductively gained and objectively applied foundation cannot be sentimental, nor can it cloud the judgment. It can only add the force of enthusiasm or consciously aroused courage to the inductively acquired understanding.

What Karl Kautsky and Eduard Bernstein wrote in their introduction to "Die Vorléiufer des Neueren Sozialismus" about the attitude of the modern socialist toward the precursors of the modern revolutionary movement, applies in my opinion to the attitude of the modern socialist toward all rebels of the laboring classes of all ages: "A deep sympathy must unite him with those who wanted to accomplish similar things, and aspired to the same goal, as he. The fact that they aimed at socialist ideals at a time when society did not yet develop out of itself the means to realize them, that they aimed at the impossible and failed, must rather strengthen his sympathies for them, for these sympathies are naturally on the side of all oppressed and downtrodden. And if he must see, in addition, that the vanquished are insulted, maligned, and befouled, not only by the victors, but also by the partisan historians, to this day, then his ire and hatred against the slanderers will fan the flames of his sympathy for the slandered so much higher. But however strong this may be and express itself, it does not stand in the way of a search for truth; on the contrary, his great sympathy for those who went before him is for the modern socialist an additional reason to devote himself to a deep study of them; and it is clear, that it will be easier for a socialist than for a bourgeois writer to grasp and understand the emotional and thought life of previous socialists."

When we realize why the laboring classes of the past attempted the impossible and failed, and when out of sympathy with them we think and speak as they themselves thought and spoke, we need neither forget the peculiarities of their historical conditions nor overlook the wide chasm which separates our feelings and thoughts from theirs. We can then estimate the historical value of things, not on the impulse of subjective, but of class feeling, not by the light of sentimentalism, but of a naturally and historically developed situation, not in the blind passion which fails to discriminate between the historically necessary and the subjectively possible, but with a full realization of both historical and subjective necessities and possibilities. The science of Socialism does not stand emotionless above, but full of life within, the class struggles, draws its vigor and power from the living process, and shares all its emotions with a full realization of their absolute and relative necessity. And for this reason my little work reflects not merely dry facts, but also the emotional side, which is as much a fact as all other inductively perceived facts of life, and which we interpret from the point of view of inductive science.

The historical line of thought accounts for the presence of several chapters and occasional passages which are not ordinarily found in works on economics. These chapters and passages are nevertheless a dialectic necessity for one who wishes to understand the growth of human societies out of animal beginnings and the interaction of economic processes with thought processes. They touch upon points which have been the subjects of much discussion among advanced thinkers, and which will occupy the center of scientific research for many years to come.

The form of presentation is my own. The economic theories belong to Marx. The method applied is that of historical materialism, supplemented in essential points by the dialectic monism of Josef Dietzgen.

In short, this little volume presents only the results of Marxian analyses. It does not epitomize these analyses themselves. Whoever wishes to find detailed proofs for the different positions taken here, must turn to the original work of Marx.

Chapter 1   What Is Capital?

Open any textbook on economics current in schools under the present system, and you will learn from it that the capital of a primitive savage consisted of a sharpened stick, a canoe, a spear, a bow and arrows, etc. Such a savage, we are told, became a capitalist by thrift, enterprise, business ability, and other so-called virtues of the capitalist world. The others, who did not become capitalists, were a shiftless lot, and their offspring have remained shiftless to this very day, and will still be shiftless when Gabriel's trumpet will call their souls to heaven — or to the other place.

Take, for instance, the conception of capital in vogue among the followers of Henry George, who is acclaimed by many as a champion of the working class.

A savage finds a fruit tree in full bearing. If he eats all the fruit, he merely satisfies his present needs. He is just a common savage. But if he eats only a part of the fruit, and, thinking of his future desires, plants another part of it, or exchanges it with other savages for other desirable things, he is a capitalist. There you have Henry George's idea of capital and capitalists in a nut-shell.

Or, take W. Roscher, a German economist, who at one time was considered a great authority on this subject by the official world of Europe. His capitalist, like Henry George's, does not even need as much "capital" as a sharpened stick.

"Imagine a fishing people without private property in land and without capital, who live naked in caves and subsist on sea fish, which, being left behind by the receding tide in pools, are caught with the bare hands. Let all laborers be equal here, and let each one catch three fishes per day and eat them. Now some prudent man reduces his consumption to two fishes per day for 100 days, and then utilizes the stored-up supply of 100 fishes to devote his whole labor-power for 50 days to the making of a boat and fishing net. By the help of this capital he catches from now on 30 fishes per day."

Has Roscher ever caught any fish and stored them in a cave for 100 days, or 150 days, in a climate where people go naked? Any American country boy can tell him that this "capital" would be a putrid mass in less than a week. Has Roscher ever subsisted on two fresh fishes per day? Has he ever tried to build a boat with his bare fists and to subsist on two rotten fishes per day while building it?

There is certainly one striking resemblance between this primitive "capitalist" and some modern capitalists. Roscher's savage capitalist makes capital out of rotten fish. Some modem capitalists make capital out of rotten beef, shoddy drygoods, poisoned groceries, etc. In this respect Roscher has indeed shown a deep insight into the character of capitalists. But there is at least one redeeming feature about Roscher's capitalist—he eats his rotten fish himself and does his own work into the bargain.

Modern capitalists are not so crude. Civilization has taught them that a truly refined capitalist does not consume his rotten goods, but labels them with fancy names and sells them to unsuspecting people at high prices. Neither does a civilized capitalist do his own work. He has surrounded himself with the halo of a representative of "The Almighty" and persuaded the working people that it is their mission to produce profits for their superiors.

Roscher, Henry George, and other vulgar economists, as Karl Marx dubs them, look upon a primitive savage with the eyes of a nineteenth century Anglo-Saxon. They see parallels which never existed. And they very conveniently overlook distinctions which are due to different epochs, different social conditions, different stages of human development. Above all, they have not one word of explanation that would show to what different social conditions are due.

To them, capitalists have existed from the days of the famous expulsion of Adam and Eve from paradise. And no matter what changes in tools, machinery, methods of production may occur, there will be capitalists till the Golden Age shall establish the Brotherhood of Men.

Taking them at their own word, how do George, Roscher, and others like them, explain the change from the self-supporting savage "capitalist" to the non-producing and parasitical captain of industry?

Thrift, business ability, etc., etc. The ridiculous rigmarole of business virtues explains it all. A man becomes a capitalist because he wants to be one, and the others down to the billionth generation are poor and dependent through their own fault. And if you ask what gives to one the will to be thrifty and enterprising and to the other to be thriftless and lazy, you get the clinching answer that "The Almighty" made them so.

But then it isn't their own fault, is it? Well, er—er—ah, you see, The Almighty—

Yes, I see. And I want to ask a few more questions.

A savage finds a fruit tree. What kind of a savage, and what kind of a fruit tree? Does the tree belong to him, just because he finds it? Do the other savages respect his claim to the sole possession of that tree? And if they do, what have they to offer in exchange for his fruit? When and how did they conceive the idea of exchange? On what basis do they exchange?

The answers which you will get to these questions will end in some more er—er—ahs.

Roscher's savage lives on rotten fish. He is naked. His only tools are his bare hands.

Suddenly an inspiration comes to him, evidently from "The Almighty." He sees before his mind's eye a boat and a fishing net. He has never heard of these things before nor had an idea how they look. Now he suddenly resolves to lay aside one fish per day for 100 days, and then to build a boat and knit a fishing net.

This is a queer savage. A naked savage with no other tools but his bare fists and living on raw fish would never think of storing any of them for 100 days. In the first place, he would know from experience that they won't keep so long. Here Roscher credits him with too little experience. In the second place, such a savage cannot count as far as 100. Here Roscher credits him with too much experience.

Furthermore, a savage living in such a low stage knows nothing of boats or fishing nets. Here Roscher credits him with a prophetic intelligence which reaches far beyond the horizon of this stage.

Before a savage of this stage can conceive the idea of a boat, he must have at least fire and a sharp stone ax. But if he had these, he would not be obliged to eat his fish raw or to live naked in caves.

Neither does a savage of this stage jump overnight into a boat-and-fish-net stage. Boats and fishing nets are very complicated inventions. Before savages arrive at their conception, thousands of years of savagery have passed away. And if we attempt to find out by what means the higher stages are reached, we must leave the sphere of speculative nursery tales and get down to searching historical study.

The first thing we learn in this study is not only to see superficial similarities, or general resemblances, but also to make relative distinctions. We learn above all to discard the self-interested capitalist point of view, or the inherited and traditional prejudices which block the way to an unbiased investigation of social problems. We no longer set up speculative theories before we have any tangible materials. We get the materials first, and out of the actual facts found by direct touch we make our theories. We fit our theories to actual things, and do not try to squeeze actual things into the strait-jacket of pre-conceived theories.

We use the so-called inductive method of research. We proceed from concrete facts to abstract theories. Then we combine things dialectically. This means that we look upon the world and society as things in the making, not as fixed and rigid. We trace out the interrelations of actual things side by side and successively in space and time, note their general similarities and typical differences, and draw general conclusions, or theories, from these interrelations. Then we apply these theories in their turn to the actual things, and in this way we test them continually as we would a multiplication by the well-known division test.

The typical mark of dialectic thought is that it reflects things in the making as a process of struggle for survival, in which the better adapted prevail over the less adapted and carry them forward to a higher form by overcoming and assimilating them.

It is from this point of view that we look upon capital and capitalist production.

We want to know the typical marks of capital. The official economists give us vague answers that explain nothing, but rather require more explanations. These men simply repeat the current capitalist notions and build economic theories out of them.

The one tells us that any tool is capital. In this way we learn that a savage of the Tertiary age, who cracked nuts with a stone, was a capitalist. But why stop at a savage? Monkeys also use stones for cracking nuts. In fact, mankind inherited the habit from monkeys. Monkeys are therefore also capitalists. This sort of economics is at best only monkey economics.

Another tells us that capital is stored-up labor. In that case the bees and ants are also capitalists. Still another tells us that capital is the fruit of abstinence. Then we get down to the rotten fish of Roscher's capitalist. Others, again, teach that capital is wealth used to produce more wealth. By wealth they mean any useful article, and by producing wealth they mean exchanging it for more than it is worth or for something that is worth more. This brings us to the cunning savage, who exchanges his fruit with other savages for things that are "worth more" to him, and this explanation ends in the story of that famous village whose inhabitants became capitalists by cheating one another at bargains.

Finally we meet the smartest of all economists, who knows that he is selling his brain, and who brings capital right home to us by demonstrating that brains, a good voice, a fine face, a good figure, are capital. This leads to the prostitute who uses her sex as capital and to the politician whose capital is his "honor."

Clearly such explanations are only make-shifts dictated by embarrassment. They explain neither the meaning of a tool, nor of a hoard, nor of wealth, nor of exchange, nor of capital. They ignore, belittle, or under-value the main things, namely labor and the different social conditions under which it is applied. They are elusive and intangible abstractions, which impress the despairing student of economics with the settled conviction that economics is indeed "a dismal science."

After reading his way through one hundred thousand pages of such economics, the student will still exclaim doubtfully: "What is capital ?"

Chapter 2   Labor And Capital

"In the beginning was Work . . . All things were made by it; and without it was not anything made that was made. In it was life; and the life was the light of men."

This is the gospel according to John.

Oh, yes, I know that it doesn't read that way now. But I also know that John was a working man. And the gentlemen who now claim the exclusive privilege of interpreting the scripture of John and other ancient working men, whose leader was killed because he differed about the interpretation of some still more ancient scriptures of some still more ancient working men with the gentlemen of his time, have never been able to give me any satisfactory reason why a modern working man like myself should not follow the good example of his ancient fellow workers and differ with the modern gentlemen interpreters. Until further notice I shall assume that a working man is more apt to understand another working man than the gentlemen are, especially when we both differ with the gentlemen interpreters about the meaning of the scriptures because we differ with them about a question of privileges. I think I am all the more justified in taking this position, because the gentlemen interpreters have always shown a very remarkable ability for distorting the clear statements of working people into obscure lies. And we have their own word for it, that John and his fellow workers noticed the same peculiarity in the gentlemen interpreters of their time.

I have already indicated that the gentlemen interpreters of our time, here in the United States, have been suspiciously quick in distorting the clear statements of Marx after the illustrious model of the gentlemen interpreters of Europe. They have been in an awful hurry to get distorted versions of Marxian theories before the American people. But not a finger have they raised to get Marx's own version of his theories into the hands of American readers, although they are continually prating about a "square deal." They have funds enough, but not one cent to spare for the publication of any work by Marx. On the contrary, they organize societies and spend millions of dollars for the purpose of giving the working people the "double cross" instead of a "square deal." They have plenty of money to publish scab papers like "The Open Shop." They can spend millions for a National Economic League, a Corporations' Auxiliary Company, a Citizen's Industrial Alliance, a National Civic Federation, all of which have but one purpose, the destruction or emasculation of bona fide labor organizations and the enslavement of the working class.

Can you see through a brick wall, when there is a hole in it? There is a big hole in the reasoning of the gentlemen interpreters, a deep chasm between their professed love for you and their battle cry of the "Open Shop," a yawning abyss between their solicitude for your education and their frenzied efforts to prevent you from learning the truth about the actual relations between your labor and their wealth.

Ancient working people like John rose up against the idea, imported from priest-ruled Egypt, that work was the wage of sin. They declared that work was life, not death, a blessing, not a curse. They demanded that work should be shared by all, not imposed as a divine curse upon the many by a few privileged, who claimed exemption from it by the grace of divine will.

The modern working people rise up against the idea, inherited from ancient and medieval rulers, that work is an inferior and degrading activity, that another thing, called capital, is the superior of labor, that the producing class should be compelled to yield the largest and best part of their product to the idle owners of the thing called capital. They demand that work shall be shared by all, and that the thing called capital shall cease to exist.

If I wanted to use the confusing jargon of the gentlemen interpreters, I might feel tempted to say that labor is the only righteous form of capital. But I won't. This is too beautifully mystic. It might be interpreted into the very opposite of what I mean. It isn't safe for a working man, who is struggling to get out of the ensnaring obscurity of traditional thought, to use such obscuring language. It would be the easiest thing in the world for one of those smart gentlemen interpreters, whose specialty it is to twist snares for untrained minds, to distort this unity of labor-capital into a new sling for the unsuspecting.

Has not the most ancient civilization in the world, the East Indian, been instrumental in distorting the natural unity of the infinite universe into a mystic supernatural unity of a "world soul"? Has it not made of a simple and natural division of social labor a mystic division of castes with different degrees of "souls"? Has it not attempted to perpetuate this graduation of "souls" infinitely and to secure a natural class rule on top of the economic one by breeding strains of these different "souls" and forbidding any intermixture of strains on penalty of death, or loss of caste worse than death? Has it not attempted to pervert the natural law of sexual selection into an instrument for damning all "inferior souls" to eternal slavery on earth? Has it not devised the most effective plan for perpetually dividing an oppressed working class against itself and rendering any united revolt of the exploited impossible?

A host of publications, radical on the surface, but reactionary in the core, disport themselves on this treacherous ground, and serve as sounding boards for the "art" of a motley crowd of Bohemian intellectuals who flirt with the revolution, but eschew all direct contact with its proletarian elements for fear of rubbing the bloom off their refined sensibilities. But this caste-like exclusiveness does not prevent them from aspiring to leadership in the proletarian revolution.

What a feast this unity of labor-capital would be for them! I can hear them rapturously declaiming: "Capital is Labor, Labor is Capital. All is one, one is all. I am the doubter and the doubt, I am the capitalist and the laborer, I am the creditor and the debtor, I am the spleen and the spleeny, etc., etc."

All of which is true enough, provided we understand that this means at bottom nothing but that all these things go to make up the natural universe.

But that is just what our mystic teachers and their friends of the ruling class don't want us to understand.

Before long the National Economic League would issue a new book on the "Cosmic Unity of Capital and Labor."

No, thank you. With all due respect for the unity of all things, I shall not forget that this unity is expressed in some very decided differences. I am not averse to a monistic reconciliation of Labor and Capital. On the contrary, I am working to bring it about. But I beg my readers to make a note of the fact that the first indispensable requirement for such a unity is the abolition of the relation between exploiters and exploited in general, and between capitalists and wage workers in particular.

Right there is the rub. Capital is not a mere thing. It is fundamentally an economic relationship between an exploiting and an exploited class. Without class rule, capital as an economic category has no existence.

Land may be capital. Tools may be capital. Articles of consumption and raw materials may be capital.

But none of these things are capital, unless they are stamped with the typical mark of capital. That mark is that these things must be means to rob the laborer of the products of his toil. Labor, and labor-power, can never be capital in the hands of the laborer. So long as the relationship of capital and labor exists, labor is always the exploited part.

It is very convenient for the exploiting class, to define capital as "wealth used to produce more wealth". So long as you don't tell who produced the wealth and under what conditions it is produced, and who gets it, that phrase is harmless. It is equally harmless to define capital as "stored up labor". The dangerous question is: Whose labor, and stored up for whose benefit and by what means?

In short, the things used as capital are not in themselves capital. They may become capital only under certain very definite social conditions, under which different economic classes struggle for the control of the products of labor.

It is on this rock that we split from the official economists, who conceal the secret of capital by ignoring the main source from which it springs, the exploitation of the labor of the working classes.

This is the source of capital. But the source alone is not enough to impress a thing with the trademark of capital. Something else is needed. There have been epochs, in which working classes were exploited, and yet they were not exploited by capital.

This other requirement is trade. The products of labor must be sold at a profit, in order that the means of exploitation may assume the character of capital.

These two essential points are neglected by the official economists. And not satisfied with slighting two such typical marks, they further complicate matters by imagining that a man can create value and accumulate capital by mere buying and selling. This is the natural result of their mistake of overlooking the part played by the labor of the working classes in the creation of values.

After having spread a protecting gloom over the secret source of capital and the methods by which value is realized in trade, economists like George and Roscher make confusion worse confounded by ignoring the historical and economic distinctions of capitals in various epochs and in different spheres. They apply conceptions belonging to one epoch to a different kind of capital in another epoch, or confound different kinds of capital working together in the same epoch by applying to all of them without distinction the same terms.

In this way they make it impossible to find any clue to the fundamental causes of social development, and to race the course of social advance along definite lines, which permit a scientific forecast of its future and outcome.

Having spread gloom and confusion all along his path, muddled several generations of students, and plugged up the avenue to scientific results in political economy, a man like Henry George climbs upon a self-made pedestal, throws out his chest, and boasts of having "recast political economy." Recast, perhaps, but only in the same old mould which safeguards the interests of caste.

The Marxian analyses, on the other hand, throw down all barriers which obstruct the emancipation of the working class from class rule. They open wide the gate of secure knowledge, which demonstrates that in the beginning was labor, not capital, and that in due time capital will disappear again, leaving the field to work, the life and light of men.

Chapter 3   Animal And Human Societies

Uncounted thousands of years before the ancient prehistoric traditions of the Jewish tribes gave rise to the myths of Adam and Eve, bands of hairy man-like creatures were roving through the primeval forests.

These creatures resembled one another in their general physical structure and general modes of life. Yet they were different from one another in some particular peculiarities.

Some built rough nests in tree tops. These passed all their lives in trees. Only on rare occasions did they come down on the ground. They hunted, ate, slept, married, propagated, and died in trees. They found all their necessities in trees. Various wild fruits, such as acorns, nuts, berries, were within the tree zone above the ground. So were young birds, birds' eggs, insects, young squirrels, lizards, etc. Even water was found in broad-leaved parasitic plants growing on the branches of the trees, or in the axles of the branches, or in the hollows of their bark.

These tree-dwelling creatures were very hairy. Even their faces and foreheads were covered with hair. Their arms were very long, excellently adapted to the tree life and its gymnastic requirements. The overdevelopment of their arms and shoulders had resulted in an underdevelopment of their legs and hips. Their legs had but thin calves and thighs, and instead of feet they had hands, by which they could anchor themselves securely to the branches of trees while reaching with their long arms for food and for new support.

Others used caves for shelter. These lived mostly on the ground, although they were also good climbers and had four hands like their tree-dwelling relatives. But their arms were not so monstrously long, and their hips and legs were stronger and heavier than those of the tree-dwellers. They walked frequently erect, using sticks to balance themselves. They lived in groups, while the tree-dwellers lived generally in pairs. They had a wider range than the tree-dwellers. The tree-folk could only climb trees well, but were clumsy on the ground. The cave-dwellers could climb trees and also hunt on the ground and run. They used clubs and stones to kill small animals, such as snakes, ground hogs, rabbits, squirrels, birds. There were more and larger beasts of prey living; on the ground than in the tree tops. The tree-dwellers were a match for nearly every animal which they might meet on their rambles through the tree tops. They could move faster from branch to branch than any giant snake, and jump higher from tree to tree than any leopard. Swiftness was their best defense against these beasts. And they were stronger than any of the smaller beasts of prey that lived on the trees.

The cave-dwellers had to be on guard against all the large hunting beasts, such as lions, sabre-toothed tigers, bears. Some of these beasts also lived in caves or prowled through them. The cave-dwellers could not live in any large cave which did not offer plenty of narrow side lanes or ledges and nooks high out of reach of prowling beasts. Only swift running and jumping or climbing to a safe place out of reach of these could save a surprised cave-dweller. But their group life made it easier for them to guard against surprises, and their numbers enabled them to defend themselves better and to scare beasts away.

The wider range of the cave-dwellers gave them a wider experience. It bred different qualities in them than in the tree-dwellers. Their different experiences expressed themselves visibly in different physical marks. Their obvious likeness revealed a common descent. Their differences showed that long adaptation to different environments had drawn them apart.

Through the same locality which these two hairy creatures inhabited, there roamed still another creature very much like them in many respects, and yet more different from them than the cave-people were from the tree-folk. This third creature was also very hairy, but its hair was so fine that the skin showed through it everywhere except on the top of the head, the back of the neck, the lower part of the face, the breast, and the lower part of the trunk. The forehead of this creature as well as his face were covered with such fine hair that the skin seemed quite naked. The hair on his head was very long and shiny. His limbs and body were even more proportionate than those of the cave-dwellers. Especially his legs were more symmetrically developed, with fleshier calves and thighs, and instead of the lower hands he had feet with toes instead of fingers.

A modern naturalist comparing these three would at once call the first two apes and the third men.

But they were more nearly alike, in spite of their marked differences, than men and apes are nowadays.

The apes were more man-like. The men were more ape-like. Particularly the young of all three creatures resembled one another strikingly.

Compared with modern men, those primitive men would be considered little better than apes. Yet they had all the essential marks which distinguish men from apes. Only in one respect did their faces resemble those of the apes and differ from those of modern men. Like the apes, they had big bony bumps over the eyebrows. But their jaws and mouth were smaller and more delicate than those of the apes.

Yet their peculiar physical differences from the apes carried with them peculiar differences in their modes of life. It was not so much the fact that tree-apes had long arms, cave-apes better proportioned arms and legs, and men hands and feet, which differentiated the modes of life of men and apes most deeply, although these external physical differences were significant enough in their way. Nor was it the fact that both men and cave-apes were social, while the tree-apes were unsocial. It was rather the different capacity of their skulls and brains which decided the relative superiority of these three types.

Evidently the external physical differences were closely interwoven with the internal organization of their brains. What had at first been but a slight variation between children of the same parents, and had predisposed each one of them for some particular mode of life or feat under the same material conditions, had gradually been sifted by natural selection and by a continued use of these variations in their particular way, until three distinct types had been created. The selection and continued use of long arms had resulted in the creation of the tree-type of apes. The more symmetrical arms and legs had created the cave-type of apes. And the larger brain capacity with a tendency to better developed legs had created the man-type with feet instead of hind hands.

The natural selection of brain qualities gave to cave-men an immense start over the apes, who differed from their ancestors only by an adaptation of some external organs to different environments.

Any changes sifted out by natural selection in any of them are directly transmitted to the offspring through the genetic processes. An uninterrupted exchange takes place between them. This intercourse is not stopped by the meeting of male and female sex-plasms at conception, but rather intensified. It continues right in the mother's womb. It shapes the brain and other plasmatic processes within the mother while the child is taking on form in the womb. Whatever produces variations in the proto-plasmatic bridges of the mother exerts its influence also on the child's plasma during formation. Natural selection is thus directly at work on the plasma, even before the child is born. [*Editor's note: At the time this was written, in 1907, the existence of genes and DNA was completely unknown, and the process of biological evolution through natural selection was very poorly understood.*]

The strongest impulse for plasmatic variations comes from the interaction of the plasmatic processes themselves. The professors would say it requires atomic metabolism as well as molecular aggregation. This means it requires changes in quality as well as in quantity. We won't go into this more deeply here, because this is primarily a work on economics, and I mention these biological matters only because they have a definite bearing upon Marxian economics. (Ever since Auguste Comte attempted to make of sociology a sort of transcendental biology, Marxians have had to contend against a confusion of biological with economic laws of development. Particularly the advent of Darwin's natural selection theory and of Spencer's theory of a social organism brought this tendency to the fore and crowded the markets with a multitude of works on biological sociology and sociological biology. Now these terms may signify a very important and valuable contribution to science. But when they purport to be a biological synthesis of

Darwinism and Marxism, they meet with the just opposition of Marxian scholars, because they amount in practice to an attempt to conceal the specific laws of social development and to a pretense that the social laws are identical with the laws of biological development. We want to understand that organic society and organic nature, while alike in general respects, have their own specific laws of development. We must be clear in our minds about the differences of social laws from biological ones. Marx discovered the laws of social development, Darwin discovered in the law of natural selection one of the most significant laws of biological development, and Spencer elaborated the theory of general evolution in various aspects, but often without a clear comprehension of specific distinctions. We want to give to Marxism its dues as well as to Darwinism and Spencerism. Of course, this does not prevent us from making a dialectic synthesis of Marxism, Darwinism and Spencerism. In fact, Marx himself has done that here and there. But it must be understood that dialectic synthesis, unlike a biological synthesis, does not confuse economic and biological laws, but distinguishes them and studies them in their mutual interactions. A dialectic synthesis need not fear to take a hint from a biological law and use it in the study of economic phenomena, nor need it fear to take a hint from an economic law and use it in the study of biological phenomena. But whoever does so, must be aware of the specific distinctions and general similarities of Marxism, Darwinism, and proletarian dialectics, and must keep in mind the impression produced by a careless interchange of these methods on a student not well conversant with either of them.)

Of course, the plasmatnc processes are also affected in quality and quantity by external influences, such as heat, cold, exertion, over-exertion (of the whole body or of certain organs). But these external processes do not produce as deep and as rapid changes as the internal processes themselves.

The external processes merely assist or retard the distribution of proto-plasmatic quantities or the alterations in the quality of plasmatic processes, which are due to the mutual interaction of these processes themselves.

On the other hand, the cave-men had acquired a plasmatic variation in their brains. It is true that this required also a somatic variation of their skulls. But whether the original impulse was somatic or plasmatic is beyond our inquiry, for it is certain that this tendency did not begin with the apes. Plasmatic variations in the direction of a superior brain and nerve system begin very low down in the scale of animal organisms, and they continue until they reach their highest summit in the brain and nerve system of man. The apes also bore the evidence of this evolution in their brains. But natural selection had not accentuated this variation in their brains any further, while in the brains of men it had done so. This accounts for the fact that this variation was so much more vital and effective than the primarily somatic variations of external organs of apes. It accounts for the biological backwardness and stability of the ape types.

The brain variation gave to men a far better control over their natural environment than to apes. It opened greater possibilities of development for men than for apes. Natural selection placed men close to the line of progressive evolution, while it forced apes into a closed alley by their somatic variations. The apes had to spend their surplus-energy in developing long arms, or legs fit for climbing and jumping, or they had to waste it in the inconsequential and meandering mode of life of their kind, to which their brain organization condemned them. It tended more to dissipate than to concentrate their brain power. But the surplus-energy of men found its typical and most effective outlet in the concentration of brain faculties, a development which carried an evolution of millions of years' duration further forward. Every use of the specific adaptations of apes welded them but more firmly to their plane, while it took men more and more away from the ape level and lifted them more rapidly to the man plane.

Of course, men did not always concentrate their minds, nor did they always use their brains in the direction of further concentration, On the contrary, they often relapsed into the inconsequential and incoherent ape-manner of thought, and we can notice this retrogressive tendency in many people even in our time. But looking over thousands of years of human development, we can plainly observe, that there has been a growing tendency to brain concentration and a greater and greater conscious effort to follow the line of understood development consistently. (The full significance of this point is not clearly brought out in any Darwinian work, because it cannot be realized without an understanding of the effects of class-consciousness on the mind of proletarian thinkers. On the other hand, no Marxian writer has so far shown the importance of a clear grasp of the thread of phylogenetic development for the elaboration of a scientific outline of human ethics. The fact that ethics are based upon common needs and vary with social systems has been sufficiently emphasized. It has also been shown, for instance by Karl Kautsky in his "Ethics and the Materialist Conception of History," that the biological origin of ethics must be sought in animal instincts. But the peculiar relation of brain development to ethics and of a conscious adaptation to a scientific standard of ethics under different social systems has not been revealed so far. I can but indicate this fact here, but this is not the place to dwell further on it.)

Cave-men and cave-apes lived under practically the same conditions. But the possession of a larger brain capacity enabled the cavemen to make more of the same environment than the apes could.

The cavemen could think better. They could remember things better and learned to express their thoughts in articulated speech. This enabled them to compare their mutual experiences better and to use them more consciously than the apes for an improvement of their living conditions.

The peculiar mental ability of the men was the original cause which differentiated human societies from animal societies. But it did not remain the only one. It produced specific economic causes, which did not only intensify the differences between human and animal societies, but which gave a still stronger impulse to the brain variation of men.

The apes would pick up sticks and stones and use them as weapons. So would the men. But the men could think about these things longer, more deeply, and more connectedly. After handling sticks and stones for a long while, the men would find out that some sticks and stones were better suited for particular purposes than others. And they would select the sticks and stones best suited for their purposes, fit them together, and try experiments with them. They would take a forked stick and fasten a jagged stone in the fork by means of flexible fiber. They would dry the skins of animals and cut them into strips by means of sharp stones or shells. They would use these strips of skin as thongs to fasten differently shaped shells and stones to sticks and try them at various uses. They would take a flexible bough, a strip of skin or animal guts, and make a bow of them. They would fasten a sharp pointed stone to a straight stick and make a spear or an arrow of them. They would take flexible grass or fiber and weave baskets and mats out of them. They would take clay or mud and plaster their baskets with it, so that they would hold water the same as gourds.

The apes could use gourds. But they could not make any dishes. They could use sticks and stones, but they could not make a spear, a hatchet, a bow, or an arrow.

The apes fled when lightning struck a tree and set the woods afire. The men fled also, when first such a thing happened in their experience. The apes would return out of curiosity to such spots and poke around in the hot ashes or glowing embers. So would the men. But the men would also pick up burning sticks, carry them to their shelters, and put more sticks on them, to keep the fire burning. They would warm their caves with the fire, drive the bear and the sabretooth out of their caves with it, and keep wild beasts away with it at night. (I do not mean to convey the impression that this was the only way in which fire was discovered. There were many other ways. For instance, it was inevitable that fire should be accidentally kindled by drilling holes in wood when making tools. It is not so much a question of discovering fire, as of learning the art of using and making it at will.) They would roast animals over the fire and put tubers into the hot ashes. They would build fire-places of stones or clay, and put clay-plastered wickerwork dishes over these fire-places to boil water and tubers. They would make animal skins, large leaves, or fiber, into wraps, aprons, or blankets.

It is quite obvious that the superior economic development of the men was due primarily to their superior brain development. The apes were held within a narrower horizon by the shape of their skulls and the texture and convolutions of their brains. Once that the physiological development, by force of natural selection, had taken this turn, there was no more escape from it. Natural selection and use would intensify it more and more. A tree-ape might be forced from a tree-life into a cave-life by some natural cataclysm, and this might lead to a more balanced development of arms and legs in his offspring, if the change of environment lasted long enough. But it would not alter the brain development of these apes so much that they would become men. On the other hand, a cave-man might be forced into a tree-life, yet this would not deprive him of his superior brain or of his technical inventions. It would simply compel him to put his brain to work devising different inventions. It would not depress his brain to the level of a tree-ape.

It is quite evident, then, that these three types did not represent any economic classes, but biological species. Nor do we find any trace of any economic class division within these three species. No amount of individual variation within these species produced any economic classes.

On the other hand, we see that biological development may, indeed, produce different economic environments.

Just in what respects biological and economic development differ, we may observe here, where they first become differentiated among the offspring of the same common ancestors. And at the same time, we may observe in what respect they are connected.

We see on one hand that natural selection produces biological variations, and that these biological variations enable one species to produce economic variation by improving certain gifts of nature and making tools. We see on the other hand, that natural selection produces biological variations, which prevent another species from making any tools.

But the making of tools, and the transformation of modes of production by further changes in tools, is the main cause of all further social progress among human beings. It is not only the cause of social progress, but induces also further biological progress, or, in some cases, retards and reverses biological processes. It is the evolution of human tools and modes of production which shapes the evolution of all other social institutions among men and determines the general course of their mental development. In short, it is the evolution of tools and of the modes of production going with certain tools, which makes what we call human history.

It is absurd to look for any economic terms among animal societies that have neither the ability to create things denoted by these terms nor the ability to express them. Where biological faculties dominate the social life more than the slight and rudimentary activity, which can be called economic only by an enormous stretch of the imagination, we need not look for any economic development in the sense that we use this term with reference to men. Picking up sticks and stones for immediate use, building nests, using gourds, etc., are activities, which do not appreciably alter the social life of the animals that perform them. These activities give no impulse to further activities which may be in any way considered as technical progress or changes in the modes of production due to technical improvements. If we want to call such activities production, we must at least understand that it is a production with natural means, not an economic production determined by technical improvements.

It is equally absurd to insist on a biological classification of terms which are derived from economic development and which denote things and processes that are in essential respects different from biological ones. We need not deny that the same general laws permeate society as well as nature outside of it, and that therefore the same general terms may be applied to social and natural development. But where entirely new forces have grown up through technical improvements and have started a series of transformations which are unique since they are not found anywhere else in the world than in human societies, no clear thinker will persist in ascertaining the laws of such social development by biological analyses. ("Just as Darwin discovered the law of development in organic nature, so Marx discovered the law of development in human society." Frederick Engels at the open grave of Marx.)

But it is not enough to differentiate clearly between biological and economic laws. A one-sided cultivation of either side is disastrous. Men remain under the influence of biological as well as economic laws, and only a close observation of their mutual interaction and of their relations to other natural laws in the entire cosmic process can give us a full understanding of all questions, which the human race must solve in its struggle for the mastery of the forces that determine its life and progress.

Chapter 4   Biological And Economic Division Of Labor

The first separation of the descendants of the same common ancestors into animal and human societies was due to biological development, as we have seen in chapter 3. It was their biological superiority which enabled men to invent and fashion tools, thereby laying the foundation for the development of economic forces, which should widen the chasm between animal and human societies.

"Technical progress forms from then on the basis of the entire development of mankind."

Lewis H. Morgan, who revolutionized the study of anthropology by his masterly work "Ancient Society," divided the development of human societies into three great stages, Savagery, Barbarism, and Civilization, according to the technical improvements made by human beings. Savagery and Barbarism were subdivided by him, each into a lower, a middle, and a higher stage, according to new tools or technical inventions introduced by men.

Important as this technical progress was for the uplift of humanity from animal-dom, yet for a long time it did not reach deeply enough down into the biological foundation of human society to make the economic forces dominant over the biological ones.

All through the stage of savagery, for uncounted thousands of years, and well into the middle stage of barbarism, biological characters formed the natural basis for the most primitive differentiation of biological from economic division of labor. The sexual division between males and females became in human societies the basis for the first economic division of labor between men and women.

This primitive division of labor between the two sexes is still found among human tribes living in the stages of savagery and barbarism. It existed among American Indians of those stages, when Columbus and his immediate followers set foot upon the American continent.

Frederick Engels, using the material furnished by Lewis H. Morgan, describes this economic division of labor between men and women in the Indian tribes of America in these words: "The division of labor was quite primitive. The work was simply divided between the two sexes. The men went to war, hunted, fished, provided the raw material for food and the tools necessary for these pursuits. The women cared for the house and prepared food and clothing. They cooked, weaved, sewed. Each sex was master of its own field of activity; the men in the forest, the women in the house. Each sex also owned the tools made and used by it; the men were the owners of the weapons, of the hunting and fishing tackle, the women of the household goods and utensils".

This is the only form of economic division of labor in human societies, which is based upon biological characters. It gives way in the transition from the middle stage to the higher stage of barbarism to further economic divisions of labor, which are no longer based on biological, but on economic causes. To the extent that this primitive division of social labor yielded to other forms, the biological division of labor became subordinated to the economic division of labor, and the female sex itself fell a victim of this shifting from a biological to an economic basis.

"Woman is the first human being, which fell into servitude. Woman became a slave, before any other slave existed . . . All social dependence and oppression are rooted in economic dependence of the oppressed upon the oppressor."

The middle stage of barbarism begins with the domestication of animals. The care and breeding of cattle belonged to the sphere of the men. Since each sex owned the things which it produced, the ownership of the herds gave to men an increasing amount of wealth, and with it greater power compared to the women. At the same time, the cattle needed wide areas for pastures, and the more herds increased, and the more at the same time the number of members of the families and other primitive organizations grew, the old territories of the tribes became too small for them. Men outgrew their primitive limits, and with them they also outgrew the primitive organizations.

"The segregation of cattle-raising tribes from the rest of the barbarians constitutes the first great division of social labor . . . Out of the first great division of social labor arose the first great division of society into two classes: masters and servants, exploiters and exploited."

The transition stage from the middle to the higher form of barbarism, then, is that stage in which human societies assume all those characters which differentiate their economics most typically from these of animal societies. Here, then, is the best opportunity to compare social division of labor among animals and men.

Long before the separation of cattle-raising tribes from other human tribes took place, other economic divisions of labor had sprung up by the side of that between the sexes. But these other divisions of social labor had not touched the biological basis of the primitive division of social labor between the two sexes.

For instance, when men learned to improve their crude stone tools by chipping and sharpening them, there were some individuals in the various tribes who developed a special skill in this line and who were assigned to this task and exempted from all other labor in the tribe.

The arrowheads used by the American Indians were fashioned by special craftsmen. "Every tribe has its factory in which these arrowheads are made, and in those only certain adepts are able or allowed to make them for the use of the tribe."

"They have some who follow only making of Bowes, some Arrows, some Dishes (and the women make all their earthen vessels), some follow fishing, some hunting."

It is quite evident that this specialization and division of labor, which takes place side by side with the division of labor between sexes and concerns only the men, is not based on any biological differentiation of men. It is not due to the fact that the arrow-makers, or fishers, or hunters, have developed different physiological organs, but to the fact that they have acquired a special skill in applying the same organs to different economic tasks. It is indeed a skill in which biological faculties are called into play by economic conditions, but the economic element is here already assuming a greater significance than any biological organ.

It is at this point that divergences between animal and human divisions of labor become very palpable. In the lowest stage of human development, this divergence is not so plain. But even here we can plainly observe a distinction between the biological functions of the sexes, and the economic functions which fall on the shoulders of each sex.

So far as sex distinctions carry with them different economic functions, economic and biological division of labor among animals is the same as that among human beings. In this respect, we have no reason to disagree with Haeckel, when he says: "The wild people, who have halted on the lowest stage to this day, lack culture as well as a division of labor, or it is limited, as among most animals, to the different occupations of the two sexes."

But right here this bourgeois spokesman of Darwinism begins to confuse sexual and economic division of labor and to build the most absurd analogies upon this confusion. Two pages further along we read: "There are many species of animals among whom the division of labor of socially combined individuals, the same as among the lowest savages, is limited to its simplest form, to the different occupations and development of the two sexes, to marriage. But there are also many species of animals among whom the division of labor of the individuals combined in societies goes much farther, and even leads to the organization of those higher social combinations, which we designate by the term states."

Here we are left completely in the dark as to what is due to biological, and what to economic "occupation and development." The term "marriage" is made to serve for both. And this obliteration of typical distinctions in one term, which denotes primarily sexual functions, offers a convenient opportunity to extend the same vagueness to the term "states" and to wipe out all essential marks of differentiation between human and animal societies —at least on paper.

Now, the social division of labor among animals living in "states" is due to biological variation. Darwin has already pointed this out very clearly. "The advantage of diversification of structure in the inhabitants of the same region is, in fact, the same as that of the physiological division of labor in the organs of the same animal body." All naturalists who have made a special study of animal societies, have dwelt minutely on the organic differences which are the basis of the social division of labor in them.

Take for instance the leaf-cutting ants in central South America, called *Oecodoma cephalates*. "The workers of this species are of three orders. The main body is formed by a small-sized order of workers with small heads. The large workers are of two kinds, one having a smooth polished head, with ocelli upon the vortex (eyes upon the forehead); the other, subterranean, having no ocelli, and, according to Bates, "fulfilling, in the depths of the colony, some unknown function."

This unknown function, it is claimed by recent explorers, consists in tending mushroom gardens. But this only by the way, for it does not affect the point in which we are interested here.

What is true of these ants, applies to ants in general. And not only to ants, but to all insect societies having any social division of labor. Every textbook on natural history describes the different orders. For instance, the societies of bees are "monarchies," those of ants "republics." But in either case, biological variation determines the form of these societies. Queen bees, drones, and workers are of organically different structure and equipped with different specialized organs. The queen bee is equipped only for the duties of conception and the laying of eggs. The drone cannot perform any other social function but that of fertilizing the queen. The worker alone has organs for gathering flower dust, honey, and manufacturing wax.

Of course, Haeckel knows this better than I do. In fact, he says himself: "Divergence of character is called by Darwin, in the fourth chapter of his famous work on 'The Origin of Species,' that mode of division of labor, which takes place between the individuals of one and the same species living together in the same locality, and which leads in their struggle for existence to the formation of varieties and later to new species. This 'divergence of character' among individuals rests as a morphological process upon the physiological division of labor, just as does the so-called 'differentiation of organs,' which is the principal subject of anatomy." And his work contains some beautifully clear illustrations showing precisely this organic difference of the orders in the animal division of labor.

But he quotes no proof, either in words or in pictures, which would demonstrate that economic classes in human societies, and human "states," are based on any physiological differentiation, which once for all assigns a definite task to human beings. A beggar has the same physiological organization as a king. It is a favorite trick of kings in fairy tales, to disguise themselves as beggars and win the love of a beggar's daughter. That could never happen in any ant or bee "state." A human queen is not prevented by any physiological organization from performing the same work as a washer woman. Whoever has been in Samoa, knows that he can get his clothes washed by some throneless queens. And various historians tell us that some modern washer women have become queens, even in Europe, and that the comparison has been by no means in favor of the queens of "royal" blood. We have but to look at the weakling on the Russian throne, the nervous Hohenzollern, the obese ruler of England, in order to know that these men do not hold their exalted position by virtue of any physiological superiority. Happy Hooligan and Uncle Tom are in many respects better men than they. Men like Rockefeller, Baer, Morgan, are by no means physically or mentally distinguished types. I can find thousands of better bodies and brighter minds among the white and colored workers of the United States. In fact, the only claim which Baer and his colleagues can advance for their hold upon the natural and social forces is that they have a deed for them from "the Almighty." But not one of them has so far produced this wonderful document, signed by the Holy Ghost and countersigned by St. Peter.

The human drones, like the bee drones, do indeed devote themselves mainly to the propagation of the species. But they cannot advance the same excuse for it as the bees. On the contrary, the human race would as a rule be much better off, if the human drones did not propagate their kind. Aside from the economic injuries which they inflict upon human societies, they leave in their sexual trail a host of cripples, insane, congenital criminals, and monstrosities.

A queen bee might with full justification call herself "the mother of the nation." She produces not only queens, but also drones and workers. On the other hand, some of the workers have the comfortable faculty of being able to propagate their kind without the help of the males (drones). The human working women are not so fortunate, and the human queens are not so motherly.

Haeckel does not only pass these palpable biological facts in silence, although he is well aware of them, but he further blemishes his Darwinian training by suppressing the fact that the working bees have a revolution once a year, in which the drones do not fare as well as the human drones will fare when the working people will have their revolution. Neither does it seem to occur to him that the queen bee discreetly leaves her hive when the first young queen bee is about to be born, and that any queen bee born after the first one is at once killed by the first-born, if she does not succeed in quickly leaving the "state." Would that human queens were so considerate!

Not enough with overlooking all these physiological differences between human and animal division of labor, Haeckel fails completely to note the economic differences which give rise to classes and different economic systems in human societies. And he does not pay the least heed to the biological facts, which he himself mentions and which should bring home to him, the Darwinian, the obvious fact, that such biological variations do not exist among human beings, and that, therefore, he should look for other than biological explanations.

"There are, by the way, some species of ants, in which all workers have become soldiers, and which have thus realized the modern ideal of human culture, the modern military state. These military states are then compelled either to let slaves perform the domestic work, or live only by robbery and pillage. This last is done, for instance, by the ill-famed South American robber ants of the genus *Eciton*. Here, again, we meet in each species with four different forms, with winged males and females and two kinds of wingless workers of very different form and size. The smaller workers, who constitute the main body of the entire *Eciton* state, all serve as privates. But the larger workers, who are distinguished by a very large head and immense mandibles, command the army as officers. There is generally one officer to a company of thirty privates."

If the human officers did not carry padded uniforms and shoulder-straps, and if they were not backed up by the whole force of tradition and official power of the ruling class, they would neither distinguish themselves from the privates nor have any power to command.

"Still far more remarkable than the military states of the Brazilian *Ecitons* are the slave states, or so-called Amazon states, formed by several of our indigenous species of ants, particularly by the blood-red and the blond ant (*Formica rufa* and *Formica rufescens*). Among these ants we find only three orders, namely, but one order of wingless workers besides the winged males and females. These workers do not labor themselves, but they rob from the nests of other species of ants (generally smaller black ants) the pupae, which they raise and which have to perform all work in the nest of the strangers as slaves. . . Thus we find among the Amazon states of the German ants the same relation of slavery which was ended only by the last war in the human states of North America."

Here we have a so-called Darwinian justification of human slavery on the ground that the slaves are of an "inferior race." But not an inkling of understanding for the economic causes, which alone made slavery possible among human beings and which abolished it. Not a sign of even a feeble glimmering of the truth, which Adam Smith had already known, that "in reality the difference of natural talents between individuals is much less than is supposed. These dispositions so different, which seem to distinguish the men of different professions when they arrive at mature age, are not so much the cause as the effect of the division of labor." Not a whisper of the plain truth, which any one can see without being a Darwinian, and which Karl Marx expressed in the words: "In principle a porter differs less from a philosopher than a mastiff does from a greyhound. It is the division of labor which has placed an abyss between the two." And this division of labor is due to economic, not to biological variations.

In the same way in which Haeckel neglects the force of economic variations in human societies, does he slight the significance of their absence among animals. He throws all such specific distinctions to the dogs and sees only general similarities.

"The history of civilization among human beings teaches us that the ascending development of civilization is connected with three different processes, namely, 1) Association of the individuals in a community; 2) Division of labor (ergonomy) of the social persons and consequently their different development, or differentiation of forms (polymorphism); 3) Centralization, or integration of the unified whole, strict organization of the community. The same fundamental laws of sociology apply equally to all other formations of communities in the organic world; also to the graduated development of individual organs out of the tissues and cell clubs. The formation of human states immediately joins the formation of herds among the mammals most related to them. The herds of monkeys and of hoofed animals, the packs of wolves and droves of horses, the flocks of birds, often ruled by a leader, show us the different stages of 'formation of states'; likewise the swarms of higher arthropods (insects, crustaceans), particularly the states of ants, termites, the hives of bees, etc."

Association in herds, swarms, flocks or in nations, states, provinces, cities; division into organic orders or economic classes; division of labor between biological orders or economic classes and trades, in nests and hives or in factories and shops; slavery through physiological causes or slavery, feudalism, capitalism due to technical causes; centralization of biological functions or of political and economic functions; organic community of interests or class antagonisms; fundamental laws of universal development and their specific form in biology and sociology . . . what does all this matter to a bourgeois Darwinian, so long as he can use vague analogies to blindfold himself and others and shut out disagreeable facts?

What would Haeckel say of a proletarian thinker who would mix biological facts as recklessly together as he does economic facts? The limits of cognition of bourgeois Darwinians are reached as soon as human history comes under discussion.

Where bourgeois Darwinism fears to tread, and where bourgeois political economy has failed, there proletarian science takes up the thread and advances without fear of consequences.

"The anatomy of civic society is to be sought in political economy."

These words reveal a secret, which neither bourgeois political economists nor bourgeois Darwinists have grasped to this day. If bourgeois Darwinians make a pretense of looking down upon political economy and denying that it is a science, they may settle that point with their bourgeois colleagues, to whom it applies. It ceased to be a fact, however, when Marx came upon the scene with his work. He made a science of political economy, and he based it upon so secure a foundation, that there is now less purely theoretical speculation and more certainty of results in this field than there is in that of biology and natural sciences in general, where scientists still operate with some very vague and unproven theories.

Bourgeois Darwinians may make a note of this.

Marx discovered the specific laws of social development among human beings. He laid bare the specific distinction of economic division of labor from biological division of labor. But while doing this, it never occurred to him to disregard the results of Darwin's work. On the contrary, he knew the art of combining Darwin's results with his own, without doing violence to either.

Read, for instance, the following passage: "the conversion of fractional work into the life-calling of one man, corresponds to the tendency shown by earlier societies to make trades hereditary; either to petrify them into castes, or whenever definite historical conditions beget in the individual a tendency to vary in a manner incompatible with the nature of castes, to ossify them into guilds. Castes and guilds arise from the action of the same natural law that regulates the differentiation of plants and animals into species and varieties, except that, when a certain degree of development is reached, the heredity of castes and the exclusiveness of guilds are ordained as a law of society."

Marx says here in plain words that the hereditary transmission of some special skill from generation to generation produced certain professional groups in the same way that natural selection transmits certain differentiations among animals and plants and creates new species or varieties, and that, when this stage of development has been reached, a social law steps in and petrifies these natural groups into castes or ossifies them into guilds. He makes a dialectic use of Darwinism and his own economic theories.

Yet this passage, and similar ones, have been interpreted by some bourgeois Darwinians as proofs for the biological basis of economics, and elaborated into the grotesque conception that economic classes, and even value and surplus-value, are "biological categories."

So far as the above passage from Marx, and similar ones, offer any ground for reserve, they do so only on their biological, not on their economic side. And this is not the fault of Marxian, but of Darwinian theories. It is doubtful whether technical skill is transmitted by heredity, or, if it is, Darwinism has not yet given a clear explanation of the interaction of plasmatic and somatic processes by which this must be accomplished.

But the economic theories of Marx have stood the test and have not been shaken in their fundamentals by any revisionism inside of the Socialist camp or bourgeois critics outside of it. That is more than bourgeois Darwinism can claim for itself.

No "biological synthesis" will ever show how economic classes are formed and economic systems transformed. Marx's economic theories, on the other hand, have clearly revealed the way in which technical advance transforms modes of production, creates new economic classes and new economic categories, produces different political institutions, molds marriage relations and laws and forces the entire physiological and thought life of mankind into definite directions. And so far as his work has been supplemented by some of his co-workers and followers, it has not been weakened, but strengthened.

Chapter 5   Societies Without Capital

It is an everlasting pity that Henry George and Roscher never had an opportunity to test their theory of savage "capitalists" by actual experience among savages. It would have been as effective in demonstrating to them the difference between grey theory and green practice as the dull thud of a policeman's club upon the head of a striking laborer is in demonstrating the difference between a sentimental identity of interests and an actual class struggle.

George would have discovered in a very short time that savages may worship many idols, but that the idol of private property in fruit trees, and of private property in natural wealth in general, was not one of them.

Roscher would have found that building a boat and knitting a fishing net with his bare hands, which implies getting the material for these things from the wilderness with his bare hands, is not as easy as sitting in his grandfather's easy-chair with felt slippers and a long pipe and writing about it. Of course, no savage would have asked him to "divide up" his "capital" of rotten fish with the rest of the tribe. But if Roscher could have accomplished the miracle of building a boat and knitting a fishing net with his bare fists, it would have taken more than professorial flubdub to convince his savages that the boat and net were not made for the whole tribe.

George and Roscher might have shouted for the police and for injunctions and militia till they were black in the face. The savages would have looked at them with pity and concluded that both George and Roscher had wheels in their heads. In this respect they would have been nearer the truth than most of their followers in modern times.

No matter in what historical or prehistorical period we investigate the social life of men up to the middle stage of barbarism, we find that they knew no other private property but that in small personal belongings, but that even in this respect there was no strict attempt to prevent others from making use of another's weapons, skins, dishes, etc. We find that land, boats, fishing nets, tents, etc., were common property, if not always in fact, then at least in principle, always subject to the common vote.

But even if George would have been permitted to pick "his" fruit tree, and Roscher to manufacture and take charge of "his" boat and fishing net, they would have been convinced with lightning rapidity, and without any "recasting" of political economy, that this was by common consent merely a primitive form of division of labor. It would have meant simply that these were their particular jobs, assigned to them in consideration of their special skill, and that they were expected to "exchange" the fruit of their labor with that of the labor of other members of the tribe without any of that haggling and mean shenanigans which go with "capital." They might have continued this sort of exchange to the end of time without being able to save up a farthing of "capital."

These are facts which had been well established long before either George or Roscher swaggered upon the scene with all the bravado of scientific quacks. Any one aspiring to the right of being classed as an ordinary scientist, let alone one aspiring to the distinction of being the scientific economist, should have had these and similar facts at his fingers' ends before opening his mouth on the subject of political economy. And so long as their followers persist in bringing forward such claims, contrary to all canons of fairness and equity assumed to be valid even in bourgeois ethics, their masters are fair game for those whose historical work is attacked or obstructed by such bogus science.

In primitive human societies, no man thinks of renting any land, trees, caves, tents, tools, etc., to another. No one produces anything with the idea of selling it. Above all, no man tries to make of production or exchange a means of getting a "profit" out of any other member of his tribe. In the most primitive stages, the tribes did not even have any use for captured enemies. They had no use for them as slaves. They could only kill them or adopt them as equals in their sex organizations (*gentes*). If Haeckel had paid just one wee mite of attention to this long known fact of anthropology, he would have had a glimpse of the truth, that mere physiological superiority is not always and everywhere a justification for making slaves of inferior types of people. And then his grotesque analogy between animal and human slave "states" would never have disgraced the pages of scientific literature.

Within each tribe, land, tools, weapons, etc., were not capital, but just means of production. Caves, tents, huts, were not means of exploitation, but just shelter. Nuts, tubers, fish, venison, domestic animals, etc., were not commodities for sale, but articles of consumption or use. And so long as there was no production for sale based on the exploitation of one economic class by another, there was no capital.

Society was then still on an overwhelmingly natural basis. The biological processes, and the division of social labor based on sex division, overshadowed the productive activity, even when other forms of economic division of labor of men ran side by side with it, and the whole weight of the struggle against nature pressed upon this primitive social formation. Blood kinship was the red bond which held the groups together, and no economic antagonism could arise on this primitive basis and disrupt the intimate bonds of social life.

This is not a soil from which capital can spring. Before any such relations as those of capital can arise, the bonds of blood kinship must be loosened and severed, the productivity of labor must be increased, and production for consumption must give way wholly or for the greater part to production for exchange at a profit.

"Capital with its accompanying relations springs up from an economic soil that is the product of a long process of development. The productiveness of labor that serves as its foundation and starting point, is a gift, not of nature, but of a history embracing thousands of centuries." (Karl Marx, Capital, Vol. 1)

The annalists of the European nations, with their ephemeral records, never saw beyond the tips of their dust-sprinkled noses. That such a thing as a human development from a lower stage than civilization, and lasting hundreds of thousands of years before the time recorded by the Bible, should ever have existed, seemed preposterous to them. Yet the more we become familiar with the records of Oriental nations, the more we find that the facts now unearthed by geologists, ethnologists, anthropologists, and paleontologists, as the latest results of modern science, were known, even if only in a mythical form, to the historians of the Indians and Chinese.

It is the fashion in certain circles to pooh-pooh the idea of a society of tree people and cave people as much as one million years ago. Even many modern scientists, who are considered great authorities in measuring historical periods, have tried to reduce this period to from 200,000 to 100,000 years. Yet in the annals of the Chinese, men are supposed to have existed two millions of years before Confucius, who lived about 500 years before Christ. Among some modern scientists, the idea of tree people and fire people, which Lewis H. Morgan has first systematically classified, and which has since been more and more strengthened by the results of geological and ethnological discoveries, is still flouted as a scientific fable, in spite of all the palpable facts which establish these things well beyond the realm of mere theories. Yet these stages are chronicled in the form of legends in the Chinese annals, without the supernatural mysteries thrown about the early beginnings of man by the Jewish records. Yew Shaou-She (The Nest-Having) is credited with teaching people to build huts in trees, and Suy-Lin-She (The Fire-Producer), his successor, is credited with the discovery of fire. The discovery of iron and the invention of the plow are laid before the great flood by the Chinese historians. The only thing which shows the hand of the ruling class in these Chinese legends is that these discoveries and inventions are attributed to individual rulers, instead of to the common labor of consanguine clansmen. But they are not surrounded by that supernatural halo which is stamped so offensively upon the pages of Occidental records.

What has been glorified for two milleniums of Christian civilization as divine wisdom and a revelation of a supernatural love, is proclaimed as a natural doctrine of ethics in clear and undogmatical language in the writings of Confucius. In fact, Confucius has not only anticipated Christ, but also the great materialist philosophers of the bourgeoisie. In many respects he was closer to what we are now compelled to defend as the positive outcome of philosophy and the epochmaking achievement of our revolutionary dialectic monist Josef Dietzgen, than most of the spokesmen of bourgeois materialism. (In his "Great Learning," Confucius has written a primitive materialist conception of society, and anticipated the French materialists of the 18th century. In his "Doctrine of the Mean," he has given a materialist outline of the mind and anticipated Hume and Kant. In his "Analects," he has anticipated Christ. "The teachings of Confucius are a system of individual, social, and political Ethics, not of Religion, in the ordinary acceptation of the term. Five centuries before Jesus appeared upon earth, Confucius gave utterance to the precise thought of the Golden Rule, and in very nearly the same words. Having been asked, 'Is there not one word which may serve as a rule of practice for all one's life?' Confucius replied: 'Is not Reciprocity such a word? What you do not want done to yourself do not do to others.' (Analects, Book XV.) But there is nowhere any clear indication that he recognized the existence of a Supreme Being, the Ruler of all things . . . . His philosophy, whether found in his own writings, or in the records of his oral teachings, as handed down in the Analects, relates wholly to the life that now is." (The Ridpath Library of Universal Literature, vol. VI) Of course, all of the statements of Confucius are necessarily vague, and merely assertive without proof. But nevertheless they express very clearly a tendency to dwell on natural facts rather than introspective speculations.

What the ancient Chinese knew and expressed in language which a child can grasp, has been muddled and mutilated by the Indian mystics, Grecian idealist philosophers, Christian theologians and bourgeois philosophers. Everywhere the revamped edition of the Jewish Jehovah has left its blurring imprint, and so it is no wonder that we find it even in the pages of so sombre and dismal a science as bourgeois political economy.

Capital is supposed to be a mystic something, which creates profit out of nothing by some alchemy of its own. The productivity of labor, this great impelling force of social progress, instead of being recognized as the creator of capital, is regarded as the creature of capital. The laborer, this veritable social creator, is hitched to the yoke of his own creation, and the drone, the capitalist, rides supinely upon creator and creation as a ruler by supernatural grace.

We will leave it to the bourgeois economists and anthropologists to settle this difficulty among themselves. For us it does not exist any longer, thanks to the work of Marx.

We know that wherever social organizations are founded upon blood kinship, where neither production for sale nor exchange for profit exists, there can be no capital. It cannot develop there, unless circumstances change, and even in the transition period to other social systems preceding modern capitalism it can develop only under exceptional circumstances and as a side-issue without any dominating power. And if we did not have all the facts of history to prove it, we should still be backed up by the testimony of every bourgeois anthropologist, who studies primitive societies at first hand. Whether we look for proof in ancient records, or in modern scientific analyses, the result is always the same. There is no such thing as capital among them.

Of course, whenever they have any sort of primitive division of labor aside from that between the two sexes, they also have exchange within the tribe or with other tribes. For such a division of labor always implies and carries with it an increase in the productivity of labor, which permits of the exemption of some members of each tribe from direct production of necessities of life, in order that they may serve the community by their special skill. But this primitive exchange lacks the typical feature of capitalist exchange, the sale of goods for profits. Particularly does it lack the whole basis of capitalist production and exchange, the "free" sale of labor-power. It is a direct exchange of goods for consumption or use, not a buying and selling for the purpose of making a profit and accumulating capital.

The American Indians knew this primitive exchange well. For instance, in Georgia the tradition has been preserved, "that among the Indians who inhabited the mountains, there was a certain number or class who devoted their time and attention to the manufacture of these darts (flint arrows). That as soon as they had prepared a general supply, they left their mountain homes and visited the sea-board and intermediate localities, exchanging their spear and arrowheads for other articles not to be readily obtained in the region where they inhabited".

This same exchange for use is still found among many primitive peoples. Quite recently Professor Frederick Starr, of Chicago university, testified to its existence among African tribes in the Congo.

He had to barter with the natives for whatever he wanted. "The best thing for small purchases," he said to a reporter of a daily, "is salt, and for large ones a piece of cloth. The cloth is in strips of eight yards, though the fathom is the unit used instead of a yard. The eight yard is a four fathom piece."

But we need not go to the most primitive peoples in order to find societies without capital. We can find very highly developed societies in ancient and modern history, which had no capital, or in which capital was just in its first stages of development and played a very insignificant role, existing barely on sufferance.

The developed states of Assyria, Babylonia, Egypt, of pre-Christian periods, were based on a co-operative production for direct use, and barter with other nations was overwhelmingly for use. The states of the Peruvian Incas, of the Mexican Aztecs, of the Natchez Indians in the Mississippi Valley, were societies without capital, without private property in land and means of production. They were societies in the middle stage of Barbarism, still held together largely by bonds of blood kinship. Wherever a conquered race had been assimilated by such societies and assigned the station of a general laboring class, the descendants of the oldest *gentes* had developed into an aristocratic hierarchy, but without any private ownership of land, laborers, or means of production. With all their division of social labor, they had not yet reached that stage in which social division of labor separates town and country into antagonistic poles.

Neither in the Grecian republic, nor in the Roman republics and empire, did anything like modern industrial capital exist. Where slave labor had become the universal basis of production, and where private property in land and means of production had become established, productivity increased sufficiently to give rise to commerce, and with it to merchants' capital and interest-bearing capital. But even so production remained overwhelmingly a production for direct use.

All through the stage of feudalism, until the beginning of the 16th century, all European states, with the exception of the rising merchant towns, were based on serf labor intended for direct use. The merchants and their capital were but froth on the surface of production for direct consumption. The medieval handicrafts in the cities acted as a check upon the development of merchants', and thus of industrial, capital.

"The rules of the guilds . . . by limiting most strictly the number of apprentices and journeymen that a single master could employ, prevented him from becoming a capitalist. Moreover, he could not employ his journey-men in any other handicraft than the one in which he was a master. The guilds zealously repelled every encroachment by the capital of the merchants, the only form of free capital with which they came in contact. A merchant could buy every kind of commodity, but labor as a commodity he could not buy." (Karl Marx, Capital, vol. 1) And so long as he could not buy the labor power of dependent men, he could not become an industrial capitalist.

It was not until the beginning of the 16th century that the conditions for the rise of industrial capital took shape, and it required the struggles of a century to pave the way for its supremacy over feudalism.

Capital, then, has not always existed. On the contrary, in the thousands of centuries of human history, it occupies but a comparatively insignificant number of centuries. And we shall see that its days are nearly numbered, and that it will soon pass into the grave of oblivion.

Chapter 6   The Rise Of Commerce

The primitive social organizations of men worked from hand to mouth, as it were. Only under very exceptional circumstances could any surplus of necessities of life be secured. When food was scarce, shelter and clothing scanty, all members of the social group suffered equally. When life was easy, all had plenty. Under no circumstances could any private individual glut himself at the expense of the others. A surplus of products could never mean lack of employment and starvation for any member of the group, as it does as a rule under capitalist production for the great majority.

Exchange of products could not assume any significance under such conditions.

But gradually the productivity of these primitive groups increases in various ways, owing to the difference in natural resources, births, division of labor, geographical and climatic changes. "There springs up naturally a division of labor, caused by differences of sex and age, a division that is consequently based on a purely physiological foundation, which division enlarges its materials by the expansion of the community, by the in crease of population, and more especially by the conflicts between different tribes, and the subjugation of one tribe by another . . . Different communities find different means of production and different means of subsistence in their natural environment. Hence their modes of production, and of living, and their products are different. It is this spontaneously developed difference which, when different communities come in contact, calls forth the mutual exchange of products, and the consequent gradual conversion of these products into commodities."

Among the American tribes, this natural basis of the division of labor is outgrown, when the llama and the turkey have become domesticated and abundant, when corn and vegetables are cultivated regularly, when various metals have been discovered and the art of fashioning them learned. Among the Indo-European races, a change comes through the domestication of cattle and horses, and segregation of stock raising tribes from the rest of the barbarians.

"The segregation of cattle-raising tribes from the rest of the barbarians constitutes the first great division of social labor ... This for the first time made a regular exchange of products possible. In former stages, exchange could only take place occasionally, and an exceptional ability in manufacturing weapons and tools may have led to a transient division of labor. For example, unquestionable remains of workshops for stone implements of the neolithic period have been found in many places. The artists who developed their ability in those shops most probably worked for the collectivity, as did the artisans of the Indian gentile order. At any rate, no other exchange than that within the tribe could exist in that stage, and even that was an exception. But after the segregation of the stock raising tribes we find all the conditions favorable to an exchange between groups of different tribes, and the further development of this mode of trading into a fixed institution." (Friederich Engels, The Origin of the Family)

Whether exchange with other tribes was, or was not, possible before the middle stage of barbarism, so much is certain that it was a still greater exception than exchange within the tribe. It could not become the rule, in the Old World, until the division of labor between stock raising and other tribes had created the prerequisites for its establishment.

Exchange with consanguine relatives within the tribe and exchange with strangers outside of the tribe, were two different propositions. To take an unfair advantage of a gentile brother was contrary to the consanguine code of morals. But it was another matter to get the best of strangers. They were considered more or less as enemies, according to the degree of friction that might exist between the tribes, and to cheat or rob them in peace or war was not only permitted, but a point of "honor."

The trading ground was in these days always on a neutral ground between contiguous tribal territories. The Anglo-Saxon *mark* (still preserved in *market*) is derived from a root which means "hunting ground", a place where wild animals lived. The traders met in these wild places, on neutral ground, away from their little village clearings, and transacted business with eyes alert and ears pricked, in the wild animal country. And they were no more watchful of wild animals than they were of one another. It was a case of Greek meeting Greek, and often enough, when bargaining became too flagrantly a cheating match, or when no bargain could be struck on account of stubbornness on both sides, the peaceful market may have been suddenly transformed into a tumultuous arena, in which men fought as fiercely over the possession of their products as wild animals fight over their prey.

The old English word *manger*, a term synonymous with "dealer", is descended from an old Aryan root meaning "to deceive", and it requires no deep penetration to realize that the cattle and horse trader of primitive times is the forbear of the modern horse swappers, who still have the reputation of being the most villainously unscrupulous and callous cheats.

The requirements of commerce have thus from the very outset played discordant melodies upon the heartstrings of the human soul. The primitive *mark* was the foretype of the modern international market, and commerce is still a disguised state of war, in which the instincts of brotherhood, bred in men by the primitive blood kinship, give way to the cunning and fierce distrust of the struggle for existence.

Modern civilization has not softened, but intensified these antagonisms. It has torn the bonds of kinship and turned the whole world, regardless of sexual relationships, into a *mark*, in which men, women, and children are taught by necessity to stifle all feelings of sympathy and to forget all the milder impulses, which religious creeds have carried down through thousands of years of history as faint echoes of a time when at least some human beings could be kind companions amid a wilderness of enemies.

Eugene V. Debs, speaking at a meeting in Hull House, in Chicago, some years ago, strikingly expressed this in the following words, to the great merriment of the fashionable ladies, who had come to hear the proletarian orator: "Look at two church deacons sitting side by side singing hymns on Sunday, and you would think they were the very soul of brotherhood. But you look at the same two deacons on Monday, when they are swapping horses, and you will get a different opinion of them. Each wants to do to the other what the other wants to do to him. That is the Golden Rule of business. And business is business."

Business and the Golden Rule are antipodes. They are not on speaking terms. Everything is fair in Love and War — and in Business. So it was in primitive exchange. It was never intended to be an exchange of equivalents. And it is not intended to be so today. All this twaddle of a fair profit is idle hypocrisy. The only fair exchange is an exchange of equivalents. And at that sort of exchange no profit can be made. None was made by any exchange within the tribe between consanguine relatives. But it was different in exchange on the *mark*, on the market, with strangers.

With the development of exchange, in the wake of the great division of social labor between tribes with different kinds of production, the ax was laid at the root of all social institutions of primitive group life.

How the development of exchange between different tribes led to the transformation of tribal business into private business and tribal property into private property, how other social divisions of labor followed in the wake of the first one, how particularly the great antagonism between agriculture and handicrafts, between country and city, arose, how slavery became an established institution, how the gentile bonds were torn asunder and brothers of the same blood divided into rulers and ruled, how the oppressive state of ruling classes was formed, all this my be read in the classic description given by Engels in his "Origin of the Family."

What interests us most here is that commerce was not, as generally represented by bourgeois historians, the great herald of peace, but on the contrary, the very principle which stimulated the most brutal passions in men and trod every gentler feeling under foot in the insatiable greed for plunder. The producing, not the trading, nations were really those who were most interested in maintaining peace, and who bred the gentlest and most generous people. Even when slavery arose among them with its inherent cruelties, it was not merciless in its exploitation, because it served only the needs of direct use, and promoted exchange with outsiders only as an incident. And even such exchange was an exchange between direct consumers.

The Peruvians and Mexicans at the time of the conquest are described as gentle and peaceful people, and they were so trusting that they fell an easy prey to the treacherous *conquistadores*, those medieval imitators of the ancient Phoenician and Grecian merchants.

It was when exchange, instead of serving the needs of direct consumers, fell into the hands of a class of parasitic middlemen, whose ruling passion was to get something for nothing by despoiling both sellers and buyers, that patriarchal servitude was turned into an instrument of torture, the patriarch transformed into a greedy tyrant, and the dawn of civilization inaugurated with such plundering, pillaging, ravishing, kidnapping, burning, as had never been witnessed before by men. Compared to the monstrous destruction spread over the face of the globe by the civilized merchant, the border warfare of the barbarian and savage tribes was mild. It was sporadic, unwillingly waged under the pressure of increasing population. It had an element of straightforward chivalry in it, which struck every close student of savage and barbarian peoples.

But the civilized trader made it his business to turn the earth into a charnel house, to leave a trail of smoking ruins in his track, to take mean advantage of the gentle and chivalrous qualities of human nature. The ancient trader bequeathed his treacherous spirit to the ruling classes, who followed after him, and with it the principle of spoils, which is still the prime incentive of all the great princes of industry.

The historical materialism of Marx has taught us that this was inevitable, and that no sentimental sniveling over things that might have been, or that might be, ever changed, or will ever change, the course of history by one hair's breadth. But in reply to the hypocritical and lying cant of the official historians and schoolmen, we point to these irrefutable facts of history as it was, and as it is, and as it will be, so long as a ruling class, driven by the economic and political laws of its system, shall march with iron heels over the gentler instincts of our race.

Chapter 7   Commodities And Money

So long as human beings produced necessities (food, clothing, shelter), made tools, weapons, implements, domesticated and raised animals, only for direct consumption and use, no question could be raised concerning any commercial properties of things. Unless a thing served some human need, or at least ministered in some way to human comfort or pleasure, it was not taken from nature's storehouse nor produced by human labor.

Neither could there be any doubt as to where all social products came from. Nature created them and human labor modified them to suit man's requirements. Labor is their father and the earth their mother, as William Petty has it.

Things had a significance only as utilities, as use-values. And so far as human labor is creator of use-values, "it is a necessary condition, independent of all forms of society, for the existence of the human race; it is an eternal nature-imposed necessity, without which there can be no material exchanges between man and nature, and therefore no life." (Karl Marx, Capital, Volume I)

But when exchange arose, first as simple barter for use, later as commerce, that is, as buying for the sake of selling at a profit, the question had to be faced: "How much of my goods shall I give for those of another, and how much shall that other give me for mine?"

And this question assumed an overwhelming importance, when commerce remained no longer a mere side-issue, compared to production for use, but when production rather became subordinate to commerce and was carried on primarily for the purposes of commerce, as it was when the bourgeois class gained control of European society to the extent that medieval feudalism was dissolved.

Now, this question concerned not so much the mere use-value of commodities, as their exchange-value. To be sure, things without use-value cannot be offered for sale as commodities, because no one will buy a thing unless he can use it. Even if the merchant himself does not care to use his commodities for his own consumption, but uses only their exchange-value, still someone must buy them for the sake of their use-value.

In primitive exchange, where use-value was directly exchanged for use-value by the producers themselves, the question of the exchange-value of the articles was not of such prime importance as it became when commerce had developed into a regular business. For the trading consumer, the use-value overshadowed the exchange-value. Here it was need pitted against need, and cunning against cunning, for the sake of getting as much use-value as possible for as little use-value as possible.

The producers, who thus exchanged their own goods, knew very well that these things were products of their own labor. The sweat of their brows was impressed upon these things and the memory of the toil expended upon them lingered with these producers. Therefore they were loath to part with their products on easy terms. What decided the point here was mainly the intensity of the mutual wants. Those who needed the offered goods most would naturally be compelled to yield a point and offer greater inducements to those who could afford to forego the coveted things without hardship. And since only such goods were offered in exchange as were not needed to supply the home demand, and only such things taken in exchange as could not be secured in the home territory, there were as many different standards of exchange as there were trading territories.

Since supply and demand thus pressed directly upon natural wants of peoples, it is quite natural that supply and demand should be considered by them as the power which determined the quantity of use-values given and taken in exchange.

But the merchant was not in the same position as the trading producers. Wherever trading nations developed, they represented comparatively small parasitic communities wedged in between large producing nations. And where the merchants developed within a producing nation as a class, they were mere leeches preying upon friend and foe in the same way as trading nations preyed upon their producing neighbors. Commodities, therefore, were not products of labor in the eyes of the merchants, but things secured by superior cunning, fraud, robbery, pillage. And these things were not secured for the sake of their use-value, but for the sake of their exchange-value. True, the use-value of things still manifested itself also to the merchants, since the supply of them or demand for them depended upon the producers and consumers who offered or wanted them. But the merchant himself cared only for the exchange-value of things. To him, therefore, supply and demand appeared as the powers which decided, not the quantity of use-value to be given or taken, but the quantity of exchange-value.

With his eyes riveted upon the exchange-value of things, the merchant came to the conclusion that this value was something mysterious, something inherent in the commodities themselves, something intrinsic to their nature. And since he did not himself labor in their production, but busied himself solely with their circulation, it seemed to him that their value, and his profit, oozed in some magic way out of their pores through his ability to strike hard bargains.

Various circumstances combined to strengthen this conception still more in the merchant's mind.

For to the extent that exchange became a regular social activity, and extended its circles more and more, overflowing its primitive tribal boundaries, breaking the ancient social bonds, and connecting home markets and international markets, the various local standards of exchange, here cattle, there salt, there shells, there metals, yielded more and more to universal commodities, which were taken as universal equivalents for all other commodities. And in the same measure in which such a universal equivalent became accepted, its use-value receded out of sight and its exchange-value seemed to be a special endowment of its material substance.

The ancient local equivalents were known to be products of social labor. But these new universal equivalents concealed their social character behind an assumed mask of intrinsic value, which they seemed to have everywhere regardless of social relations.

In this way, a universal equivalent assumes the form of money.

"The particular kind of commodity to which it sticks is at first a matter of accident. Nevertheless there are two circumstances whose influence is decisive. The money-form attaches itself either to the most important articles of exchange from outside, and these in fact are primitive and natural forms in which the exchange-value of home-products finds expressions; or else it attaches itself to the object of utility that forms, like cattle, the chief portion of indigenous alienable wealth. Nomad races are the first to develop the money-form, because all their worldly goods consist of movable objects and are therefore directly alienable; and because their mode of life, by continually bringing them into contact with foreign communities, solicits the exchange of products." (Karl Marx, Capital, volume I)

The advent of the money-form of a universal equivalent tended to deepen the mystery, which hung about the exchange-value of commodities. More than ever this value seemed to be innate in the things themselves, particularly in the money-commodity.

Still other causes accentuated this tendency.

Not every commodity is equally well adapted for the functions of money. Bulky and unwieldy things which cannot be easily passed from hand to hand and divided into suitable portions, will not be as serviceable as small and readily divisible things. Commodities which wear out quickly will not be as acceptable for the services of money as durable ones.

It was at this stage that the discovery of precious metals in large quantities filled a long felt want. Gold and silver have all the natural properties of an ideal universal equivalent. They are easily divided, easily weighed, durable, and may be circulated without difficulty. Gold and silver seemed natural money, and they gradually assumed this function to the exclusion of all other commodities.

In order to serve as money, a commodity must unite in itself the functions of a measure of value and a medium of circulation. Gold and silver were naturally fitted for this. And they had one quality, which made them particularly dear to the hearts of the merchants: they could be hoarded indefinitely without spoiling.

The exchange-value of a commodity expressed in terms of money is its price. Formerly prices were expressed in quantities of the different commodities that were exchanged for one another. In such primitive exchange, some commodities had to be measured by number, others by weight, others estimated in bulk. Gold and silver simplified the transactions of commerce, for these metals could be easily weighed in any desirable quantities required in trading, and a small weight of them represented a large value.

If the exchange-value of other commodities had assumed the mysterious form of intrinsic value in the eyes of the merchants, because the labor that created both their use-value and exchange-value took place outside of the merchants' sphere, is it a wonder that the exchange-value of gold and silver assumed this mystic form even with greater apparent force? Gold and silver were produced in the bowels of the earth in a way unknown to man, brought to light and passed from man to man by methods which often had every reason to shun inquiry. These metals were therefore the mysterious powers of value par excellence, and the exchange-values of other commodities strove for incarnation in them.

When slave labor became the established form of social production, as it did in the ancient civilization on the borders of the Mediterranean Sea and in Asia, the mysterious nature of value was shrouded in so much greater obscurity. For the slaves were not considered worthy of recognition as human beings, and their labor was not measured in terms of any value. So the exchange-value of commodities, and particularly of gold and silver, was gradually accepted as its own mysterious product, not only by the merchants, but by the people in general.

This was the state of affairs when the desire to control the movements of gold and silver and to facilitate their circulation gave rise to the coining of these metals. Hitherto they had been exchanged in bulk (as bullion, dust, ornaments). They had to be weighed in bulk. Now the authorities (and this meant generally the ruling potentates) stepped in and placed their hand upon the money by claiming the exclusive privilege of coining it.

So long as these metals had to be weighed in bulk, there had been at least the possibility of making the relation between the unit of price, the measure of value, and the values of commodities in general, open to inspection. So long as one ounce of gold was paid for so and so many ounces of other commodities, there was some universally known mathematical relation between gold as a unit of price, gold as a measure of value, and between this measure of value and the values of other commodities. If one ounce of gold was the unit of price, two, three, four, or more ounces could easily be expressed in terms of this unit. And if 5 ounces of gold paid for 100 pounds of dates, in other words, if the value of 100 pounds of dates was an equivalent for the value of 5 ounces of gold (by agreement if not in fact), than the value of 200 pounds of dates was measured by that of 10 ounces of gold, and so forth.

But with the coining of gold and silver, this open numerical relation between the value of gold and silver and the value of other commodities was abolished. The weight of gold and silver contained in each coin was arbitrarily fixed by the authorities, and a certain denomination of coin passed for a certain value, no matter whether that coin was newly minted or worn flat.

The unit of price was now a certain coin, and the weight of the metal in that coin bore no organic relation whatever to its value or to the value of the commodities for which it was exchanged.

The notions produced in the brains of the merchants, and of buyers and sellers generally, by this state of things were accepted as correct explanations of the true conditions underlying these surface indications. These notions were handed down from generation to generation, without much inquiry into their soundness. When the bourgeoisie required a clearer grasp of the forces that shaped themselves to bring the capitalist class into power, bourgeois political economy took up these questions and juggled with these superficial notions for three centuries, without ever getting to the bottom of the mystery.

Then Marx came upon the scene in the middle of the 19th century and declared that it was the business of science, not to accept surface indications as true explanations, but to go to the bottom of the matter and find the underlying causes of the notions which had dominated the minds of men for centuries. And he went to work discovering these causes. What he discovered we shall see in subsequent chapters.

But even after he had placed his discoveries before the world, the political economists of the ruling classes persisted in teaching the superficial and grotesque jugglery of the so-called classic economists, and in propagating notions which had been the outcome of conditions in which everything combined to obliterate the actual source of exchange-value, the labor of the producing workers. And to this day you will hear these notions dished up as great learning in the universities of the ruling classes, and you will see the gilded youths struggling laboriously to assimilate the ideas of a dead civilization, under the impression that they are being equipped to solve the problems of present society.

Chapter 8   The Development Of Merchants' Capital

Commodities and money were the materials out of which the merchants built their fortunes. These materials were permanently available for them, wherever the ancient forms of gentilism had given way definitely to private property in land and other means of production.

Not all nations of antiquity in which an aristocracy developed, opened equally favorable opportunities to the traders. Where division of labor was solidified into castes, as it was in Egypt and India, the social conditions did not offer as wide a field to the merchant as they did in Greece and Rome, with their widespread systems of free producers.

Yet it did not matter what might be the form of production, whether it were patriarchal, tribal, or carried on under a system of castes or of slavery — so long as there was a surplus of goods that were taken to the markets as commodities, the merchants found a way to make themselves at home and to establish themselves as lords of the markets.

But they could not make themselves lords of production, so long as their activity remained wholly confined to the sphere of circulation.

They could, indeed, exert a strong influence upon production, but this influence could never be a constructive one. It could only be destructive. Throughout the whole long period of its existence from primitive beginnings to the end of its independent existence in the 16th century, merchants' capital exerted essentially a dissolving influence upon the productive activities of peoples.

In the beginning, the merchants' capital merely performs the role of a middleman between spheres of production which it does not control. Even where large commercial cities or whole trading nations developed in antiquity, their commerce merely promoted exchange between the barbarian producers that surrounded them.

But to the extent that commerce extends its sphere and gains in importance, it makes its corrosive influence felt in the productive spheres which it despoils. The merchant has only one aim — to make a profit by buying and selling. To buy cheaply and to sell dearly is the secret of his wealth. Therefore he cannot and will not exchange equivalents. He buys at an arbitrary price and sells at an arbitrary price. The producers on either side may know the labor-time which their articles have cost them. But this labor-time does not express itself as a value in the price of these articles when they become commodities. The merchant does not take the labor-value of commodities into consideration at all. He simply compares the prices which he pays with the prices at which he sells. These prices are controlled by his class, so long as merchants' capital is the prevailing form of capital.

Yet even so, the merchant cannot fix prices wholly at his own sweet will. The control of the markets and of prices by his class is not a consciously directed and combined control. It is rather a result of the intermittent and undisciplined interaction of individuals following their own selfish ends and thereby exerting unconsciously a check upon each others' greed.

Even at the earliest stages of commerce, the social character of the commodities and of their own activities makes itself felt to the merchants. They may haggle over prices with producers and consumers, and imagine that there is no limit below which they cannot depress the price to the producers, and no limit above which they cannot raise the price to the buyer. But they become gradually aware that there are certain average limits above and below, beyond which they dare not venture, except on rare occasions. The lowest average limit at which they can buy is the price fixed by competition among sellers. The highest average limit at which they can sell is the price fixed by competition among merchants themselves. A merchant may manage under exceptional circumstances to make an extra profit by buying below this average or selling above it, but he soon becomes aware of the fact that there are certain forces over which he has no control and to which he must bow.

The natural result of this experience is to strengthen still more his belief in the mysterious immanent powers of value in commodities.

This social power makes itself felt to the merchant in proportion as commerce assumes its typical features under the various modes of production which he exploits. It will be more easily defied by the merchant in his dealings with such direct producers as nomadic tribes and patriarchal communes than with slave-holding aristocrats and despotic caste states. The latter have more or less the same end in view as the merchant, and look upon labor with still greater disdain than he does himself. Compared to them he is himself an inferior. Their dominant aim is the accumulation of wealth, not the exchange of commodities for the sake of using them. The only things which they are likely to covet for their own use are articles of luxury, ornaments, spices, etc. On the other hand, the primitive producers exchange things primarily with a view to obtaining articles for direct consumption, and this makes it easier for the merchant to take advantage of their needs and get the best of the bargains.

Under these circumstances, the merchants themselves, by their own activity, will gradually acquire a fair estimate of the equivalent nature of the value which they exchange. And in proportion as the social character of commodities expresses itself in the prices paid and received by the merchants, the comparison of the different prices of different markets will easily make it possible to strike a certain average between them, which will assume the aspect of the equivalent around which prices fluctuate. This equivalent may, or may not, be very near the actual labor-value of the various commodities. But this is immaterial at this stage, because labor-power it not bought and sold as a regular commodity. Its price does not bear any relation to the prices of commodities even where slaves are bought and sold, because these slaves are generally captives, are bought and sold in bulk, without any possibility of measuring the value of their labor, and perform their labor under conditions in which the money-value of their productivity cannot be easily ascertained.

Where the social division of labor between agriculture and town handicrafts promotes commerce within certain nations, it is evident that trading will exert a far greater influence upon the productive activity than it will when it is merely performing the role of a middleman between different producing nations. But in any case, its influence is always primarily negative, corrosive, destructive.

The extent to which commerce can exert its blighting influence depends largely on the stability and resistance of the various modes of production. It will not be able to reach deeply into such systems as the Egyptian and Indian castes and communes, while it transforms ordinary divisions of labor quickly into a system of slavery and tends to make of partriarchal slavery a system of slavery producing surplus-products.

Hand in hand with this internal development of commerce goes the development of usurers' capital. Once that private ownership in land has become firmly established, and commerce developed to the point where it does no longer skim the cream off occasional surplus-products, but stimulates the steady increase of surplus-production, the small land owners easily fall a prey to the money-lender. A crop failure, the death of a cow or horse, a war, suffice to deliver the small land owner gagged and bound to the money-lender.

All through antiquity we see, therefore, that merchants' capital assumes the form of commercial and financial (money-lenders') capital. But we see no other form of capital. Nowhere do we see any capital based on the direct sale and exploitation of the labor of free laborers for profit. The surplus-products which reach the markets are always an excess of production over the requirements of direct consumption, and capital plays its role as an exploiter of surplus-production wholly or overwhelmingly in the sphere of circulation.

In proportion as this development proceeds, commerce extends its rule over industry. In the pre-capitalist stages of society, commerce rules industry. The reverse is true of modern society. Of course, commerce will have more or less of a reaction on the societies, between which it is carried on. It will subject production more and more to exchange-value, by making enjoyments and subsistence more dependent upon the sale than upon the immediate use of the products. Thereby it dissolves old conditions. It increases the circulation of money. It seizes no longer merely upon the surplus of production, but corrodes production itself more and more, making entire lines of production dependent upon it. However, this dissolving effect depends to a large degree on the nature of the producing society. So long as merchants' capital promotes the exchange of products between un-developed societies, commerce does not only assume the shape of out-bargaining and cheating, but also arises largely from these methods. Leaving aside the fact that it exploits the difference in the prices of production (by price of production Marx means the cost price plus the average profit) of the various countries (and in this respect it tends to level and fix the values of commodities), those modes of production bring it about that merchants' capital appropriates to itself the overwhelming portion of the surplus-product, either in its capacity as a mediator between societies, which are as yet largely engaged in the production of use-values and for whose economic organization the sale of a portion of its product, which is transferred to the circulation, or any sale of products at their value, is of minor importance; or, because under those former modes of production, the principal owners of the surplus-product, with whom the merchant has to deal, are the slave holder, the feudal lord, the state (for instance, the oriental despot), and they represent the wealth and luxury which the merchant tries to trap, as Adam Smith has correctly scented . . . Merchants' capital in its supremacy everywhere stands for a system of robbery, and its development, among trading nations of old and new times, is always connected with plundering, piracy, snatching of slaves, conquest of colonies. See Carthage, Rome, and later the Venetians, Portuguese, Dutch, etc." (Karl Marx; Capital, vol. III)

The circulation of money is everywhere accompanied by an accumulation of money, and the hoarded money in its turn assumes its own peculiar forms of circulation as interest-bearing capital. Both commercial capital and interest-bearing capital, once that they have assumed their typical forms, pass through a long series of adaptations to different forms of production, and finally fall under the sway of industrial capital, wherever the dissolution of the old societies leads to the rise of the modern industrial capitalist.

Merchants' capital as the ruler of the sphere of circulation, exploiting the surplus-production of producers outside of its direct control, and industrial capital as the ruler of the sphere of production, buying the labor-power of its own employees in the open market like any other commodity, exploiting its employees directly in the sphere of production, carrying on production for the sole purpose of accumulating industrial capital by the subjugation of the sphere of circulation to its control, these are two significant forms of capital, each of which marks different historical epochs and the prevalence of different social systems. But you will look in vain for a characterization of these typical differences in the conceptions which the vulgar economists of the ruling classes palm off as genuine science on the unsuspecting and gullible pupils, who come to them for information.

Chapter 9   Merchants' Capital In Phoenicia And Greece

The earliest merchants who played a significant role among the nations of antiquity on the eastern borders of the Mediterranean Sea, were of Jewish descent. They had developed out of primitive nomadic tribes living on the borderland between the great barbarian societies of Assyria and Egypt. Wandering back and forth with their flocks between the Euphrates and the Nile, they formed the first chain of communication between the East and West, and blazed the first caravan routes between the great centers of population in Mesopotamia and Northeast Africa.

At the time when Assyria-Babylon and Egypt were fully matured, about 1500 B.C., these trading tribes had separated into the Phoenicians on the small belt of coast land west of the Lebanon, the Jews in the valley of the Jordan, and the Arabs on the fringes of the Arabian desert.

The influence of their different geographical environments assigned to each one of these nations a peculiar place in the commercial life of that period.

The Phoenicians, jammed into a rocky strip of coast not more than fourteen miles wide and 150 miles long as at its best, cast off their primitive social organization with a rapidity which was equaled but rarely in history.

In all of ancient history, the Ionian tribes of Greece and Asia Minor, who about 500 years later developed into the strongest commercial competitors of the Phoenicians, under similar surroundings, are the only parallel. Already in the year 1000 B.C., the Phoenicians had great and flourishing sea ports in the cities of Sidon, Tyre, and lesser towns along the coast, and not only dominated the sea trade, but also drew a large portion of the overland eastern and southern trade into their control.

The Arabs, crowded into the waste places near the desert, remained essentially nomadic. Their mode of living and social organization perpetuated itself almost unchanged from age to age, and even when at a later period the Arabian conquests carried some of these tribes into northern Africa and lifted some of them into a commercial city life, the desert tribes continued in their backward existence and organization. It is not until modern industrial capitalism expands into these out-of-the-way regions and grips them with its strangle hold, that even these fossil organizations are pressed into service, disrupted, or completely annihilated and extinguished. This has taken place in our own time, quite recently, and is still going on. The British and French invaders found these tribes still in the same conditions in which their primitive ancestors lived, when Sidon and Tyre were in their pride. Now, as then, they attended to the overland carrying trade with their "ships of the desert," acted as scouts and guards for caravans, and, last but not least, accumulated wealth by plundering each others' patrons or levying tribute upon merchants for protection.

The Jews performed the function of a half-way station from the time of the early beginnings of Phoenician commerce to the final destruction of Jerusalem by the Romans and the dispersion of the Jewish people. When the Phoenician commerce and handicrafts had already well developed and divided the Phoenician people into rulers and ruled under a political system governed by the privileged, the Jews were still overwhelmingly nomadic and agricultural in patriarchal families. Their exposed position between restless commercial and predatory tribes, great barbarian societies based on agriculture and always expanding with the increase of population, North and South, and the geographical location of their territory, which left them no outlet East and West but the sea and the desert, was not calculated to encourage settled habits and city life. Only during the breathing spells of history, as it were, did the Jews enjoy a settled life, and as soon as they did, the commercial environment was always ready to exert its corrosive influence and promote the rise of a class of privileged in league with a select hierarchy, after the model of commercial Phoenicia and of barbarian Egypt, Babylon, Assyria, Persia. What the incessant stream of caravans inaugurated in a gentle and imperceptible way by slow degrees, that was completed at one fell blow, again and again, by the invading armies that tramped through this region from north to south, and south to north, as long as the Jews existed as a nation. In such an environment, only a privileged few could accumulate spoils and wealth, and even these could escape with their spoils only under exceptional circumstances. In short, only the crafty merchant could survive here. The Jews became a tramping race of peddlers and money lenders, spreading by stealth over the entire face of the ancient and medieval world, and existing only on sufferance, but developing for this very reason a craftiness and resourcefulness which made some of them the secret rulers of the fate of nations by means of their underground accumulation of gold and silver. Runnymede might have told a different tale and produced something else than a Magna Charta, if King John could have squeezed as much gold out of his Jews as he needed, and many a modern war might have taken a different course, had the secret stream of gold from the coffers of certain Jews flowed in a different direction or stopped its flow at certain critical points. (Of course, this does not mean that mere merchants' capital made history of itself. It is always the mode of production and its technical basis and productivity, which are the fundamental causes of historical processes, and merchants' capital plays its role, however significant and far-reaching that may be, as a mere accessory to these fundamental forces.)

The commerce and city life of the Phoenicians, with its international intercourse and experience, and the impossibility of agricultural production on such territory as theirs, rapidly concentrated the energies of this nation upon intellectual pursuits and handicrafts, so that scientific exploration, voyages of discovery, and technical skill distinguished the Phoenicians above all other nations of their time. With the extension of the commercial relations necessarily came a demand for way-stations along their regular routes. In the course of the centuries, the Phoenicians planted trading posts in Cyprus and Crete, on the islands of the Aegean Sea, on the northern coast of Africa, and in southern Spain. Vast emporiums were built up at the strategic points of the overland routes to Persia and Egypt, and in the borderlands back of them. Wherever the merchant went, his armed guards went with him, and stole producers and products, if they could not buy them. A steady stream of captured slaves poured into and out of these great trading posts. The gold and pearls of the East, the ivory of Central Africa, copper from Cyprus, silver from Spain, tin from the British Isles, frankincense from the interior of Arabia, linen from Egypt, cutlery from Damascus, pottery and ornaments from Greece, leopard's, tiger's, and lion's skins from India and Africa, all passed through the hands of the Phoenician merchants, and all left a golden souvenir in their hands.

Very little of all this real wealth, which expressed itself as gold in the merchants' hands, came from the labor of the Phoenician artisans. With the exception of purple dyes and fine cutlery, the overwhelming bulk of the merchandise was the spoils of looting and cheating. And the whole vast organization rested in the last analysis on the practical or virtual slavery of the vast multitudes, who tended cattle, raised agricultural foods, spun, weaved, fashioned, dug and grubbed in caste seclusion, under hierarchic despotism, or under the supervision of armed overseers. Into this dark foundation of the barbarian societies, which the Phoenician merchant despoiled, his influence never reached far enough to alter the steady march of their productive forces. He could filch their surplus from them, or rob them even of their necessities, but the foundation of the whole social structure was not touched thereby. He might corrupt such small and fluctuating nations as the Jews, and even exert at short intervals an overwhelming influence upon them as happened at Solomon's time, but he could never move the stolid bulk of the great barbarian societies in their quiet transition to a form of civilization, which must be the inevitable outcome of their peculiar modes of production.

Neither did the merchant always have things his own way. Often the biter became the bitten. The covetousness of the rich families sooner or later led to jealousies and internecine civil wars. That is the ever-recurring story of merchant cities or merchant republics, no matter what mode of production they despoiled or in what period they lived. Only the methods of warfare changed.

Nor were the despoiled nations always quiet sufferers. The aristocratic families of the nations trading with the Phoenicians realized easily enough that the wealth piling up in Sidon and Tyre was filched from them and their laboring people, and they waited only for a favorable opportunity to fall upon the Phoenician caravans, levy tribute upon them, or invade their country.

Already in 800 B.C. the results of internal conflicts and the dread of the encroaching Assyrian power drove many wealthy families out of Phoenicia and led to the foundation of Carthage. And when Sargon and Nebuchadnezzar overwhelmed the Phoenicians and dragged their best families, like those of the Jews, off to the fields of Mesopotamia, a few of the richest Phoenician families fled to Carthage. Of those who survived and remained, many followed the same course later. After the downfall of the Babylonian rulers, Tyre became tributary to Persia, and the more the strength of the mother country waned, the higher rose the star of Carthage. When Alexander the Great swept through this region, he destroyed a large part of Tyre and gave the final blow to Phoenician power in Asia Minor. Carthage assumed the supremacy of the Mediterranean commerce.

But even before this time, other competitors had arisen on the borders of the Mediterranean Sea. While Sidon and Tyre were yet in the bloom of their prosperity, the Ionian Greeks began their rapid upward career to merchant power. And at the same time the Dorians had crossed over to Greece, one tribe to become the founders of Athens, the other of Sparta.

In this overwhelmingly insular and peninsular environment, the merchant found his natural sporting ground. Here, as previously in Phoenicia, he quickly slipped out of the shell of the gentile organizations and created a world after his own image, with slavery as the natural basis of production and commercial and financial capital as the skimming ladle. The mountain tribes and the overwhelmingly agricultural Spartans, who disdained commerce, here represented the inert and heavy mass which pulled backward just as the barbarian societies in Asia had hung to the heels of Phoenicia.

It must not be supposed that the destructive influence of merchants' capital was always a reactionary one. On the contrary, it was often a revolutionary power, and particularly in those early days of transition from a gentile constitution to a rule of privileged classes, merchants' capital, in spite of its destructive force, acted largely as the agent of social progress.

Neither must it be supposed that there would have been no transition from gentile brotherhood to class rule without the intervention of merchants' capital. Such a transition was inevitable, and came fundamentally from changes in the technical forces. Merchants' capital hastened or retarded such changes, under different circumstances.

In the transition from gentilism to class rule among the ancient Grecian tribes, merchants' capital helped to dissolve the old bonds faster and to strengthen the rising aristocratic families. Here it played a revolutionary role. Later, in the transition from feudal serfdom to capitalist manufacture, its position is reversed, and it resists, in a reactionary manner, the encroachments of industrial capital upon its domain.

Not that it is ever wholly revolutionary or wholly reactionary. Its peculiar position as a middleman compels it to be ever on the lookout for advantages on either side, and to utilize both reaction and revolution for its own ends. But when we compare long historical periods and observe the role played by merchants' capital during such long periods, we can clearly observe that its influence was more revolutionary there, more reactionary here. But under all circumstances, it never was employed by the merchants with a conscious understanding and forecast of historical tendencies. That was impossible for them. Such a knowledge is the crowning outcome of very recent discoveries. The merchants were, and still are, veritable creatures of the moment, the incarnation of the policy of momentary advantages, and the wider results of their activity in the historical process were always unpremeditated, and often undesired, by them. (In order to prevent a misinterpretation of this passage, I call the reader's attention to the fact that I make no attempt here either to condemn or to praise the merchants for any of their qualities. On the contrary, I present these qualities as simple facts, born of historical necessities. If the reader meets in this work with occasional passages which seem to imply that I judge certain facts by a standard of feeling, I wish to say by way of explanation that my standard is neither a subjective nor a sentimental one, but a historical one, acquired by the development of history itself. Since we necessarily regard human existence and a normal human development as the primal good, and everything dangerous to human life and progress as bad, and since not all historical necessities are good in this sense, it is evident that the application of the method of historical materialism itself enables us to get a birds-eye view of the prevailing good and bad tendencies of human development, and thereby to acquire a standard of appreciation which is neither subjective nor sentimental, but objectively historical and scientific.)

About 1000 years B.C., the old gentilism was still alive among the Grecian tribes. This was the heroic era of the Greeks. It was at the same time the era in which new elements made themselves felt and undermined the old social organizations. Engels sums up these elements in the following words: "Paternal law and inheritance of property by the father's children, favoring an accumulation of wealth in the family and giving to the latter a power apart from the *gens*; influence of the difference of wealth on the constitution by the formation of the first rudiments of hereditary nobility and monarchy; slavery, first limited to prisoners of war, but already paving the way to the enslavement of tribal and gentile associates; degeneration of the old feuds between tribes into a regular mode of existing by systematic plundering on land and sea for the purpose of acquiring cattle, slaves, and treasures. In short, wealth is praised and respected as the highest treasure, and the old gentile institutions are abused in order to justify the forcible robbery of wealth." (Engels, The Origin of the Family)

Even before this time, trade with different tribes on the borders of the Mediterranean had been well developed, and the surplus products of the tribes of Greece circulated as commodities in the markets of Asia. The poems of Homer, which describe the Grecian society of this stage, mention improved iron tools, blacksmiths' forges with bellows, handmills for grinding grain into flour, the potter's wheel, the preparation of oil and wine, artistic ornaments of precious metals and copper amalgamations, wagons, war chariots, merchant and war vessels, marble architecture, fortified towns, luxurious interiors of aristocratic homes and temples. In short, all the conditions necessary for the development of merchants' capital were already present among the Greeks 1000 years B.C., and since even at that time the gentile lands had been distributed among private families, there was also an opportunity for lending money on land and getting a grip on unfortunate debtors by means of interest-bearing capital in the form of mortgage on land. Also land began to be rented to colonists. Here, then, we find all the primitive forms of unearned income existing, as profits on capital in commercial enterprises, or as interest on capital invested in loans on securities, or as rent for the use of land. But here, and all through the periods of ancient slavery and medieval feudalism, these forms of unearned returns on capital operate on different economic classes and in a different manner than they do when industrial capital becomes lord of circulation and production. Under slavery and feudalism, as historical systems of production, profit, rent, and interest assume far different forms and follow far different channels than they do when propertyless wage workers sell their labor power as a commodity in the open market and produce surplus-value directly under the supervision of the capitalist with capitalistically owned machinery.

Already 600 years B.C., commercial profit, and its companions usury and rent, had completely destroyed the independence of the farmers of Attica.

"All the rural districts of Attica were crowded with mortgage columns bearing the legend that the lot on which they stood was mortgaged to such and such for so much. The fields that were not so designated had for the most part been sold on account of overdue mortgages or interest and transferred to aristocratic usurers. The farmer could thank his stars if he was granted permission to live as a tenant on one sixth of the product of his labor and to pay five sixths to his new master in the form of rent. Worse still, if the sale of the lot did not bring sufficient returns to cover the debt, or if such a debt had been contracted without a lien, then the debtor had to sell his children into slavery abroad in order to satisfy the claim of the creditor. The sale of the children by the father — that was the first fruit of paternal law and monogamy! And if that did not satisfy the bloodsuckers, they could sell the debtor himself into slavery. Such was the pleasant dawn of civilization among the people of Attica." (Engels, The Origin of the Family)

Things soon became unbearable. The debtors revolted. By the help of their political rights, they secured legislation which defended their property against that of the creditors. It was Solon, who, in 594 B.C., declared all debts illegal and restored the land to the people.

But he could not abolish the forces of social development. He could not even abolish the distinction of classes, which divided the people of Attica into rich and poor. He had to adapt his legislation to the existing conditions. And the best he could accomplish was to turn the course of development into other channels.

Since he had made speculation in land on a large scale impossible, merchants' capital found another outlet for its energies, Instead of investing their money in land, the wealthy now invested in slaves, ships, commodities of all sorts—in short, in movable property. This shifted the burden of exploitation from the citizens of Attica to the slaves and to outsiders, at least for a time.

The new commercial nobility now became the revolutionary force in Athens. They wrested more and more of the supremacy out of the hands of the old gentile aristocracy, and finally overcame them by the revolution of Cleisthenes, in 509 B.C. The downfall of the gentile aristocracy at the same time completed the ruin of the old gentile constitution.

By this time many foreign immigrants had become citizens of Athens, without however, having been adopted into the gentes. The new constitution divided all citizens regardless of gentile relations into townships according to geographical location. This definitely lifted the commercial "democracy" into the saddle. But the great mass of free citizens soon made the experience, which the American laboring classes are just making today, and which culminates in the understanding that mere political democracy without industrial democracy amounts in practice to a virtual oligarchy.

Under the old aristocratic rule, class antagonisms and distinctions in wealth had made themselves felt, indeed. But nevertheless all free citizens regardless of class interests had felt a strong interest in the welfare of the whole community. But from now on the last bonds between the old community and its members were severed, and wealth regardless of nationality asserted its power.

With the new state of affairs, merchants' capital acquired a greater power in Athens than it had ever possessed before. The merchants rose to greater and greater influence.

As in the case of Phoenicia, so in that of commercial Greece, the concentration of wealth into a few hands and the pressure of an increasing population against the national boundaries led to colonizing expeditions at an early stage. These colonies were either mere trading posts, over which the mother city retained full authority, or they were independent settlements, which might remain in a friendly connection with the home country, but administered their own affairs. The oldest Greek settlement is generally supposed to have been Cumae, founded in the vicinity of the region now occupied by Naples, Italy, about the year 1050 B.C. Various Ionian settlements, such as Naxos and Catana, were founded on the eastern shore of Sicily, while the southern and southwestern coast of this island was colonized by the Dorians. Syracuse was founded by Corinth in 734 B.C. The whole southern portion of the Italian peninsula, various islands in the Adriatic Sea, the southeastern coast of France (for instance Marseilles), and parts of the eastern coast of Spain and the northern coast of Africa, were settled by Greek colonists.

These colonists were in every essential respect the children of their mother country. They carried the mode of production, political institutions, and social customs of the home country with them, and even if they started on a lower historical foundation, they planted the germs of the same evolution. Sooner or later they developed the same general tendencies as the people at home.

The general outcome was everywhere a pauperization of the great mass of free citizens, and their depression to a level where their only chance of existence lay in competition with the despised slaves, or in begging and tramping. But it was considered ignominious for a free man to work, particularly to work under supervision.

The pauperization of the free citizens therefore spelled ruin to the whole community, and that meant the whole state.

The political rights of the beggared freemen could not save them from such a fate. Their political power could not restore to them their economic independence. What had still been possible for the debtors at Solon's time, became impossible for the dispossessed under the new regime.

People who love to speculate about things that might have been, may find an interesting puzzle in guessing what might have happened had the whole problem been simply one of internal development. We cannot follow them on this speculative excursion. We must limit ourselves to things that really happened. And for this reason we must keep in mind that not a single one of the ancient Phoenician and Grecian states and colonies lived out their own lives undisturbed by foreign interference. Whenever matters approached some climax, which might have inclined the scale of victory in favor of the oppressed classes, some foreign complication interfered and gave new power and more room for expansion to the merchant class.

In Athens, a great turning point came with the attack of the Persian power on Greece. The revolt of the Ionian colonies in Asia Minor against Persia was the danger signal, which diverted the attention of warring factions and cities from their internal troubles and rallied them all for the defense against the common enemy. From 495 B.C. to 466 B.C., the struggle lasted and was finally decided in favor of Greece. Athens became the commercial ruler of the Aegean Sea.

The economic result of this victory for the people of Attica was to make the rich still richer and the poor still poorer. The commercial interests soon imposed as heavy a yoke upon their own people as that of the hated Persians might have been. Athens became the center of looting sallies, by which nearly the entire population of the islands and coasts of the Aegean Sea was made tributary or subject to the commercial capital of that city. Spoils of war, slaves, and profits of commerce piled up as never before in Attica, the crowd of political heelers living at the public crib increased apace, and corruption spread at an alarming rate.

A new contest between democracy and commercial aristocracy became inevitable. But again foreign influences complicated the problem and came to the assistance of the plutocracy.

It was at this stage that the aristocratic constitution of Sparta, which had prevented the inroads of commercial capital among the free men of that state, asserted its reactionary influence and sent the Spartans to the aid of the aristocrats of Attica. The democratic elements, who controlled the politics of Athens and shifted the whole burden of taxation upon the shoulders of the aristocrats and rich, had long been the object of hatred among all exploiting classes, and now came an opportunity to wreak vengeance. The money-bags of Athens showed their patriotism by conspiring with the Spartan nobles to overthrow the democracy of Athens. For thirty years (431-404 B.C.) the Peloponnesian War raged, and finally ended with the temporary downfall of the Athenian democracy and the rule of Spartan tools in Attica.

And so the battle between democracy and aristocracy fluctuated back and forth. The economic result was always the same: the commercial wealth and economic power was distributed between different ruling factions, the mass of the freemen bore the brunt of the fighting, and found themselves generally in a worse condition when peace was restored than before the outbreak of hostilities. The number of paupers increased.

We need not dwell any further on the historical development of Grecian and Phoenician states. The only purpose of this brief and rapid sketch has been to show the means by which merchants' capital rose to power in ancient slave societies, how it maintained itself through all vicissitudes, and how it survived. We have seen enough to understand that it was essentially predatory, that it had no other practical means of increasing the productivity of labor than that of increasing the number of slaves, and that it was not constructive in periods of transition but principally destructive. It could make beggars of free men, but it could not make free productive laborers of them, so long as slavery remained the foundation of society. Neither had merchants' capital any power to transform slavery into a form of production which should be able to lift society out of its economic fetters into a freer level. It required forces outside of this society to bring new life into it and to extricate merchants' capital out of the slings of its own making.

Out of these historical conditions it could not escape until new forces made themselves felt. All through the further development of ancient society, we see therefore merely a reproduction of the conditions which we have just sketched. The continued struggles between the small Grecian states, the fight of Carthage and Syracuse for the commercial supremacy of the Mediterranean, the rise of Macedonia and Epirus, the growth and expansion of Rome into a world empire, all this takes place on a stage set with the same scenery, and everywhere merchants' capital plays the same role of the conscienceless and successful villain.

It has been dinned into our ears again and again that the merchant was the life and progressive force of ancient society, that democracy was the ruin of Grecian civilization, and that all the high culture of that early human development was inspired by the noble and public-spirited trader. We have shown enough of the real state of things here to prove that it was not democracy, but slavery, which undermined the ancient culture, that merchants' capital had much to do with the increase of slavery, and that its progressive power was not due to the progressive spirit and noble intentions of the merchants. A plague may also inspire Progress, and a criminal may stimulate inventive genius to great exertions. Of this nature was the progressive influence of the merchants in ancient slave societies.

Chapter 10   Merchant's Capital In Rome

In the Roman empire, we may observe on a large scale what we have just noticed on a smaller scale in the Phoenician and Grecian states and colonies. Nowhere does the inertness of slavery and the destructive influence and constructive impotence of merchants' capital spring into view so strikingly as in the last centuries of the disintegrating Roman power.

The early history of Rome, in its economic phases, is largely a counterpart of the Grecian, only modified by peculiar geographical and national conditions. The primitive transition from gentile to class organization shows little difference from that among the Dorian Greeks, only that the Roman *gentes* from the outset were under the necessity of mingling more freely with outsiders than the Greeks.

This may have been an additional help to the formation of aristocratic families, for the original *gentes* would naturally draw closer together under the necessity of maintaining their sway over the conquered Latin tribes, which remained outside of the Roman *gentes*. Very likely the commercial functions fell largely upon the shoulders of the outsiders. But in view of the absence of reliable data on this period, nothing definite can be said about the influence of commerce upon the primitive Roman organization.

So much is certain, that here as in Greece, the merchants' influence helped to break the old bonds and to create great differences in wealth, which finally led to an overthrow of the old gentile constitution and the enactment of laws by which the wealthy gained control of the economic and political power.

Within this constitution, all the struggles between plebs and patricians took place, and in these struggles the merchants' capital played the same role which it did in Greece. Here, as in Greece, the outcome was a complete pauperization of the masses. The free plebeians were first turned into debtors by means of heavy interest on money loans, then robbed of their land and transformed into slaves.

"The same wars by which the Roman patricians ruined the plebeians, by compelling them to serve as soldiers and thus preventing them from reproducing the requirements of their productive activity and making paupers of them . . . filled the sheds and cellars of the patricians with looted copper, the money of that time. Instead of giving to the plebeians directly the necessary commodities, grain, horses, cattle, they loaned to them this copper, for which they had no use themselves, and availed themselves of this condition for the purpose of enforcing enormous interest by usury, thereby turning the plebeians into their debtor slaves . . . In the Roman empire it happened frequently that famines caused the sale of children or the voluntary sale of free men by themselves into slavery to the rich." (Karl Marx, Capital, vol. III)

In the Roman Empire, this form of usury quickly defeated its own ends. In proportion as it turned freemen into slaves, it abolished farming on a small scale and introduced large scale farming on latifundian estates by means of slaves. To the same extent did loaning money on land become unprofitable. For what usury squeezes out of the small independent producer is the whole surplus product above his necessities of life (with the exception of the small portion paid to the state in taxes). But it can never squeeze the whole surplus-product out of the slave owner, the feudal lord, or the modern industrial capitalist. From the exploiting classes, it cannot get more than a portion of the surplus-product. To what extent usury will reach down into production itself, will, therefore, largely depend upon the mode of production. It can never overthrow the mode of production, which is under the control of an exploiting class. All it can do is to exist as a parasite, and to suck more or less of the surplus-product out of the exploiting classes, the same as commercial capital. Once slavery had become the prevailing basis of production in the Roman empire, commercial capital absorbed the lion's share of the spoils and usury lived on as a hunted and despised thing.

Merchants' capital, however, does not fare any better in the long run. It undermines itself the same as usury does, and languishes as soon as the mode of production reaches the end of its possibilities. In fact, all capital, no matter what its origin and methods, is its own worst enemy, its own limitation, its own gravedigger. But it does not reach the end of its tether in the same way under different modes of production. Under ancient slavery and medieval feudalism, merchants' capital vegetates in nooks and byways as soon as a critical period of transition approaches, and adapts itself to new circumstances wherever it finds a little breathing room. Under modem industrial capitalism, both industrial capital and merchants' capital undermine their own foundation for good and destroy their possibilities of existence forever.

In Phoenicia and Greece, merchants' capital always found new outlets among newly developing markets, when the old markets within a certain group or nation had become unprofitable. But in the Roman empire, merchants' capital ultimately found itself at the end of the resources of the whole international market of the European world. As the concentration of wealth and means of production proceeded, large masses of money were accumulated by a few financiers, but at the same time manufacture lost more and more of its market and fell finally far below its average level. The more of the independent artisans and farmers were expropriated, the larger became the mass of the paupers, who could not buy regularly. Just as usurer's capital loses its opportunities to the extent that chattel slaves or wage slaves take the place of independent producers, so merchants' capital loses its opportunities to the extent that the mass of paupers increases. Usurers' capital thrives best at the expense of a large mass of small producers. Commercial capital thrives best at the expense of a large host of independent consumers. In the Roman empire, the introduction of slavery as the prevailing basis of production robbed both usurers' and merchants' capital of their best customers. And to the extent that the Roman power extended its scope and dragged more and more foreign nations into the whirlpool of the Roman misery, the main springs of commerce ran dry and finally stopped flowing altogether. Only in the East, where the vast unconquered Persian and Arabian multitudes rubbed shoulders against the remnants of the antique Grecian people, a pitiful relic of the once flourishing commerce of that region continued to vegetate.

Slavery, with the vigorous assistance of merchants' and usurers' capital, had brought the Roman empire to the verge of ruin. Already at the beginning of the Christian era, the first forebodings of the coming downfall announced themselves, and as the centuries proceeded, the evidences of internal decay accumulated and broke out in leprous spots, which gradually spread over the entire complexion of that vast aggregation of nations.

Never before or after has history erected such a stupendous monument to the innate impotence of capital. Never before has the historical process shown so plainly, that the laboring, not the exploiting classes, are the salt of the earth. And if the salt decays, wherewith shall society be salted? If nations were receptive for historical object lessons, the decline and fall of the Roman empire would be a milestone looming with piercing ruggedness out of the gloom of the past and pointing with granite fingers to the warning, that there is only one sound and indestructible basis for human societies . . . the free labor of free producers on terms of economic equality for all without exception.

But nations do not learn that way. History has left its milestones for a few to study and ponder over. These may carry the germs of historical object lessons from generation to generation. But these germs will not sprout and bear fruit, until the laws of social development force the laboring class itself to act in accord with historical laws and become the conscious element of its own emancipation.

Under the conditions of the decaying Roman empire, such a consciousness could not develop among the laboring classes. We know, indeed, that the slaves were conscious of their oppressed condition and chafed under it. We know that they banded together in vast armies and fought bravely for their liberty. We have even unmistakable evidence that they had dreams of a free world. But we know also that these slaves could never succeed in abolishing slavery, could never gain control of the productive forces of their time. We know, furthermore, that the early Christian movement seized vast bodies of slaves and freemen, and rallied even Roman legions to the standard of the social revolution. We know that these Christians, like the revolutionary slaves before them, had also dreams of a free laboring world. But we know that in spite of all this, their consciousness was not the class-consciousness of the modern proletarian revolutionist, was not the outcome of an understanding of their historical mission and of the means by which this mission must be fulfilled.

Since neither commercial capital nor slave labor contained within themselves the capacities for self-emancipation from their own degenerating effects, new life could come to the decrepit Roman empire only from the outside. It came in the shape of invasions of German tribes, whose barbarian organization was still full of the vigor and health of free men. These Germans were rather hunters than agriculturists. But the conquest of Rome gave them control of vast estates, and they quickly adapted themselves to agricultural pursuits.

As used to be their custom, the German tribes parceled the former latifundian estates out among their members by *gentes* or families. They were not ashamed to work, for they had not known slavery and did not feel its degrading power. So the German tribes lifted the Roman power out of the slough into which slavery and merchants' capital had driven it. But at the same time, the resurrection of agriculture and its prevalence as the essential mode of production signified a lower stage of industrial development than the Roman empire had formerly enjoyed.

We see here a fact which has often been overlooked, namely, that mere industrial development in advance of people with lower industrial development does not necessarily imply supremacy over people in lower stages. In the scale of social evolution the Phoenicians stood higher than the Persians, the Athenians higher than the Spartans, the Romans higher than the Germans. Yet the combined influence of the self-destructive tendencies of slavery and commercial capital, and of the superior vigor of barbarian institutions, gave to people with gentile constitutions, or with vigorous relics of gentilism, the supremacy over the more highly developed societies of their neighbors. A high stage of industrial development does not always and everywhere signify a high development of the human body and mind, nor does it always and everywhere signify an inevitable transition to a higher form of society. It may or may not, according to a multitude of other circumstances, which must be determined by careful research.

The conquest of Phoenicia by Persia carried with it a decline of the Phoenician society. At the same time it insured the rise of Grecian society and its victory over Persia. The different elements in Grecian society in their turn carried Greece first forward, then backward, and finally decreed its downfall and the supremacy of the socially lower Romans. The Romans in their turn went to pieces through the forces of their own society, and had to yield the floor to the barbarian Germans. The Germans carried new life into Rome, but were in their turn infected with the same destructive virus which had ruined the Roman empire. Yet so strong was the vigor of their barbarian organization that they not only survived the downward tendencies of their new environment, but lifted it out of its depths and carried it forward into a higher stage of development. This stage was feudalism. Just how this was accomplished, we shall see in the next chapter.

Chapter 11   Merchant's Capital Under Feudalism

The German tribes who took possession of the Roman empire did not enjoy their new environment undisturbed. Hardly had they adapted themselves to the new economic conditions and settled down to agricultural pursuits, when they, in their turn, were attacked from all sides. From the North, the Normans fell upon them. Out of the East came the rush of the horsemen from the Hungarian and Russian plains. From the South and Southwest the Saracens crowded in.

Farming was not a very prosperous occupation under these circumstances. Besides, the Germans were warriors, more accustomed to the sword than to the plow. Fighting and farming did not agree very well. The German communes took but gradually to regular farming, and set aside a large portion of their lands for pastures and hunting forests. And when invasions of roving tribes disturbed these communes and compelled them to revert to the old barbarian mode of living from time to time, communal farming often took second place and cattle raising and hunting had to make up for the losses in agriculture.

While the development of communal agriculture proceeded but slowly under these adverse conditions, the development of slavery was, on the other hand, prevented by the same causes. In the first place, slavery did not agree with the gentile constitution of the German tribes. In the second place, communal agriculture signified small-scale production for immediate consumption, not for the market. Slavery as a basis of production thus became impossible. It did not disappear entirely, but it ceased to be practicable as a means for supplying a large market. For the market was gone.

Not that all trading ceased. But trade became once more mainly a simple barter of products for direct use. Money as a medium of exchange fell into desuetude among the German communes, particularly north of the Alps, where it had been barely introduced by the Roman merchants. Once again commune exchanged with commune only those things which were not needed for home consumption, and home industry once more took the place of division of labor by industrial crafts. The German women performed most of the work formerly done by skilled Roman slaves. Skins and linen were, and remained, the prevalent clothing material among these tribes. Where wool was used, it fell to the lot of the women to clean and spin it. Even as late as the 8th century the daughters of Emperor Charlemagne still had to spin wool for their father's household, and it was not until the middle of the 11th century that wool spinning developed into a manufacture outside of the house and family. This industry developed first in Flanders and Frisia, where it had already been in vogue under the Roman emperors, and where it continued to vegetate after the fall of Rome, until the social division of labor and the increase of population made a wool manufacture on an industrial scale possible. The transition of linen manufacture from the hands of the women to those of male craftsmen took a still longer time.

Commerce as a profitable business for capitalist merchants thus found very narrow limits in the transition period from Roman slavery to medieval feudalism. Only such luxuries as had become indispensable to the wealthy under Roman civilization were still brought in by merchants from the East. Otherwise it was only the Christian church that stimulated other than intercommunal trade and created a demand for ornaments, wine, incense, fine draperies, and artistic dishes.

Commercial capital could not assume any social significance in this environment. It lived its parasitic existence in humble walks, and did not receive any encouragement from the church. The communal system of production with its frugal habits and free landholders offered so little encouragement to the moneylender, that interest on money was denounced as usury by all leading churchmen of this period. Yet the church was itself the main instrument of commercial expansion in those days. The missionaries were then, as now, the advance agents of commerce. They penetrated into the little known regions of the North of Europe, made geographical and ethnological discoveries, and established missionary stations, which in due time became the centers of commerce. Very often the bishop became the chief merchant and banker of those places. For instance, Bremen was a missionary station founded in 688 A.D., Hamburg another one founded in 811. The site of Lubeck was a trading post known even at the time of Ptolemy, in the second century of the Christian era. The coast of the Baltic was opened up to commerce by the exploration of the Knights Templar. In Africa, the same mission was fulfilled by Mohammedan missionaries, who penetrated into the interior and converted savage tribes, while they blazed caravan routes, carried away slaves, and captured ivory and precious metals.

The great merchant towns in the Mediterranean, which had played a prominent role in ancient Greece and Rome, did not lose their economic significance in this stage of transition. But their trade was reduced enormously. Nevertheless, they remained centers of traffic as before. There was even sufficient trade between different sections of the European and African countries to permit of the growth of new merchant towns. Venice, for instance, was founded in 452 A.D. by Italian refugees who left Padua when the invading hordes destroyed it. The Adriatic islands offered enough opportunities for coast trade to develop Venetian commerce as early as the 6th century.

But all this was in a desultory and uncertain stage. Invasion after invasion threatened the security of the merchant and destroyed the basis of his business, the peaceful communes that sheltered the wealthy families, his principal customers.

In proportion as the continued fluctuations between settlers and warriors introduced new elements into the old communes and demanded a readjustment of their mutual relations, the tribal community of interests expressed itself in new forms, which still retained much of the mutual duties and privileges between the members of the same commune, but at the same time shifted the balance in favor of the privileges of the wealthy and prominent families. The continual wars left much land without any known owners. The invading tribes, if successful, redistributed this land in various proportions, according to the customs prevalent among them. Often the leaders received a larger share than the other members of the tribe. Where large masses of armed warriors had to be held ready for the protection of those who cultivated the soil, it became the settled custom that the tillers had to feed the warriors and their chief. Where villages grew up around such armed camps, or around fortified churches and convents, the custom soon developed to place the tillers under the protection of the armed men, or of fighting missionaries and monks, with the understanding that the tillers should supply the armed men and perform so many days of labor on the land of their chiefs.

This was the primitive basis upon which the relation between feudal lords and serfs grew up. The free peasants begot children, who in the course of the tendencies of this period found themselves depressed more and more to a level of dependence upon the lords. The armed retinue overawed them, the lord made arbitrary changes in the long established customs, enforced these changes against the resistance of the peasants by the help of his armed men, and squeezed more and more extra labor out of the serf. The church became an exploiter of the oppressed in the same way, in spite of its platonic remonstrances against the evils of class rule.

While the serfs were a dependent class, yet they were not in the same position as the slaves of ancient civilization. The slaves were strangers and captives, without any shadow of civil right. The serfs were members of the same commune, and whatever might be the privileges of the lord, he had also certain duties towards his serfs, which he could not easily shirk. The feudal organization rested in the last analysis on the organization of the serfs, and this enabled them to stem the encroachments of the nobility through class struggles, a thing which the ancient slaves could never accomplish.

Once this new relationship had become universal in the principal countries of Europe, and the invasion of barbarian hordes had become rare, the productivity of the serfs increased sufficiently to give rise to a surplus, which could be thrown upon the market and sold for money. Since not only agriculture, but also handicrafts were carried on by the serfs, the feudal villages were as self-supporting as the old *mark* communes and did not have much use for the services of the merchants. It was the kings, the nobles, the bishops, the well-to-do serfs, who could employ the unpaid labor of many, who gathered more goods than they and their non-producing retinue could consume, and who were thus able to throw a surplus of goods upon the market and trade them for luxuries and money.

Commerce and the use of money could not, therefore, become general in Europe until the number of wealthy grew and until the continued production of surplus goods made the establishment of regular market places possible. These market places gradually came into being through the development of particularly well-situated villages which were right in line with the natural courses of traffic, such as the Rhine, the Elbe, the Danube, and with the military roads built up by the Romans across the Alps and throughout the different regions of Germany and Gaul. Out of these market villages grew in due time the merchant towns, with their fortified walls and their specialized handicrafts and trading lines.

The dormant stage of commerce in the Occident during the fermenting stage of European society after the collapse of the Roman empire shifted the center of mercantile supremacy for several centuries to the Oriental countries, in which the Arabian people had gradually pushed all other nations aside and assumed the position of the ruling nation. In 622 A.D. Mohammed began his crusade, and by 634 Syria, Egypt, Northern Africa, and Spain had fallen under the sway of the Mohammedans. Their further progress north out of the Pyrenean peninsula was stopped by Charles Martel in 732. But they pushed their way across the Bosporus, captured Constantinople and gradually penetrated toward the Hungarian and Austrian countries, until they had control of the commercial lines of Eastern Europe and of Asia. With Constantinople as the key to the water routes of Eastern Europe and Asia Minor, with Baghdad as the center of the Mesopotamian land routes, with Cairo as the gate to the commerce of Eastern Africa and the various parts of North Africa and Spain, the Mohammedans were in a position to rule the Mediterranean and to hold the competition of the rising Italian merchant towns in check. In this evolution of Mohammedan commerce, the Jews played a very important role as international agents and money-changers. When the demand for Oriental articles of commerce grew among the well-to-do classes of Europe, the various merchant towns became the natural emporiums for the transit of these goods, and the rulers of Europe were only too glad to enter into diplomatic negotiations with the hated Mohammedans for the purpose of making commercial treaties with them. As early as 797, Charlemagne employed Jews as commercial agents between himself and Haroun-al-Rashid, and opened the port of Marseilles to the Mohammedan vessels. The Mohammedans, on the other hand, availed themselves of the services of such cities as Venice and Genoa on a basis of mutual concessions, and thus exerted an indirect control over their European competitors, so long as the Eastern routes were under Mohammedan sway. They even played Genoa and Venice against each other, and paid them for their services to the Mohammedan cause with money, spoils and privileges. These Italian cities, on the other hand, true to trading instincts, made similar bargains with the European plundering expeditions, called Crusades, and thus skinned wealth from both friend and foe after the manner of true capitalist patriots. Genoa retained its commercial offices in Constantinople even during the Crusades, as shown by a letter of Emir Abd-Allah to the archbishop of Pisa, in 1157, and the evidence strongly pointed to the fact that the Genoese merchants assisted the Turks against the Christian Crusaders, in the interest of "civilization."

In the course of the 13th century European conditions developed to a point where commerce became flourishing. The little market villages of the 12th century had developed in all central points into strong merchant towns, with definite privileges, which they defended against the encroachments of the nobility with all the fierceness of the money-lover. Along with commerce came the growth of a regular money business. The many different standards of coinage, the insecurity of the trading routes, the difficulty of conveying large sums of money safely to far distant places, demanded the development of credit, the establishment of reliable money-exchanges, and the emancipation of credit from the exactions of usurers and money monopolists. From this time on banking in its various phases, and the handling of money for a consideration, became a permanent feature of commercial life.

The old form of usury continued as it had under ancient slavery. But the requirements of marine commerce and the wholesale trade demanded the emancipation of the merchant from the exactions of the moneylender. Credit associations of merchants were the first forms by which the merchants secured for themselves a more flexible medium of circulation at rates of interest, which their business could bear. Out of these associations rose in due time the various state banks and the modern credit system.

"The credit associations which were established in the 12th and 14th centuries in Venice and Genoa, arose from the need of marine commerce and wholesome trade connected with it to emancipate themselves from the domination of ancient usury and from the monopolists of the money business. The fact that the bona fide banks, which were founded in those city republics, assumed at the same time the shape of institutions for public credit from which the state received loans on future tax revenues, is explained by the circumstance that the merchants forming such associations were the prominent men of those states and as much interested in emancipating their state as themselves from the exactions of usurers." (Karl Marx, Capital, Volume III)

Just as Mohammedan commerce had first dominated the Italian cities, so the Italian cities now extended their influence to the German and French markets. Along with the Jew came the Italian financier, established himself in the chief markets of Europe, and for centuries played a prominent role in European finance.

So long as small scale production for direct consumption had been unable to furnish any surplus with which the parasitic classes could carry on their competitive struggle for wealth, the ban of the church on usury would not have been necessary at all in order to make the lending of money at high rates of interest unpopular and socially unessential. The social conditions themselves were powerful enough to restrict usury to the dealings between money monopolists and wealthy spendthrifts. And now, when social conditions opened large avenues of opportunity for the moneylender, the ban of the church proved as ineffectual as it had once been unnecessary. This social power over more platonic church decrees asserted itself to such an extent that the church itself became helplessly involved in the practices of the moneylenders and accumulated immense riches through them.

"The taking of interest had been forbidden by the church. But the sale of property for the purpose of getting out of a tight place had not been forbidden. It had not even been forbidden to transfer property for a certain period to the moneylender as a security, until such time as the debtor should repay his loan, so that the moneylender might have the use of the property as a reward for the absence of his money . . . The church itself and the various corporations and communes belonging to it derived much profit from this practice, particularly during the period of the Crusades. This brought a very large portion of the national wealth into the possession of the so-called 'dead hand', all the more so because the Jews were barred from engaging in such usury, the possession of such fixed lines not being concealable. Without the ban on interest the churches and cloisters would never have become so rich." (J.G. Busch, Theoretisch-praktische Darstellung der Handlung)

The wars of the various lords and princes created a steady demand for money, and yielded rich harvests of interest to financiers. The church corporations themselves were compelled to make use of banking facilities for the same reasons. The great religious orders could not get along without credit, and the assessment of taxes for church purposes and crusades inevitably demanded the credit and banking systems. It had become the custom in the Middle Ages to levy a tax of 100 to 100,000 florins for the privilege of clothing a man with the rank of bishop. Many candidates for this office were poor men, and they either had to borrow the money from some moneylender and get it back out of their pious flocks, or to go without the honor. The collectors of the church often entrusted Italian or French bankers with the transfer of these sums, and the popes encouraged this practice. Transports of coin cost a great deal for armed escorts, and the safest way to escape taxation or loss at the hands of robber barons was to secure the services of a banker. Florence at one time had a monopoly of the papal money business. The Holy See itself had to back up the loans of its bishops, because the bishops often failed to pay their debts and the bankers refused to lend them money unless the church endorsed the loan and promised to make good any loss incurred through bad debts. It happened not infrequently that the congregations were called upon to pay the debts of their bishops, and if the flock refused, they were excommunicated. The citizens of Cologne, called upon to pay the debts of their bishop, resisted the raising of their church taxes for this purpose, and a number of other towns came under the ban of the popes for the same reason. This led in September of 1246 to the decision of Pope Innocent IV that in future the debts of bishops should be paid by their congregations only if the debts had been contracted for the benefit of the church.

This was virtually an official declaration permitting the lending of money at interest. It was an admission that money could not be gotten without interest. The next step in this direction was a systematization and facilitation of money lending to church people by the church itself. On October 25, 1288, Pope Nicolas IV issued blanks to be used by church people in their transactions with moneylenders. The debtor was permitted to bind himself, his successors in the bishop's office, and his church members, with their movable and immovable property. Interest was still under the ban officially, but the same effect was accomplished by various resorts which amounted in practice to a tacit sanction of usury.

"The slyest tricks were resorted to in order to conceal the taking of interest. It was the custom at one time to call the interest for the first six months a gift, for the second six months a gratuity. Grain and other products were taken in place of money." (Dr. Ad. Beer, Ge schichte des Welthandels)

Sometimes it was arranged that the debtor should return the capital and pay all incidental expenses, particularly expenses due to deferred payments. All this was nothing else but the payments of various rates of interest for the use of money.

The rate of interest rose naturally in proportion as the taking of interest was tabooed and the moneylender's business was risky. No general rate of interest existed during the middle ages. At the time of Charlemagne 100 percent were the limit at which usury began, and from 10 to 40 percent were ordinary averages. Emperor Frederick II decreed that Jews should not charge more than 10 percent. He said nothing about the rate which Christian money lenders (or the church itself) might take. While Jews and heretics were murdered for their independent ideas concerning religious matters, the gold and valuables belonging to these unfortunates wandered into the coffers of the church. Both the Inquisition, and later the Reformation, and the numerous persecutions of the Jews, served as potent factors in concentrating money and wealth in general in the hands of the various religious organizations.

Aside from these financial transactions with the moneylenders, the church had other means of amassing great sums of money. Pious souls hoped to earn salvation by making their fortunes over to the church. After committing all the deadly sins on the calendar, the rulers would buy their way into heaven by means of the wealth, which they had stolen and filched from the people. Others made bequests to the church in their lifetime and lived on a certain part of the interest. Sometimes the successors of these repentant sinners would break into the possessions of the church and take all they could get hold of, spend most of it in riotous living, and then crawl back at the end of their wanton lives with the remainder of the plunder and obtain forgiveness. There is more joy in heaven over the repentance of one sinner than over the upright lives of a thousand saints.

The poor, on the other hand, often fled to the armed churches for protection: just as in Greece and Rome the temples were the refuge of the persecuted, so in the Middle Ages the cloisters and churches became the refuge of the oppressed. Whole villages sought protection from their oppressors in the church and delivered their wealth over to its keeping in exchange for this protection.

With the establishment of the money system came also a juggling with the coinage and a speculation on future constellations of the money market. All through this period of the Middle Ages we meet with decrees of authorities to the effect that the laboring classes should be held within the place assigned to them by Divine Providence by paying them in depreciated coin. Already in the 14th century the legitimate fruits of money speculation were harvested in the form of bankruptcies of large firms, due to non-payment of interest and the confiscation of capitals by princes and church dignitaries. Boycotting became a favorite means of the town burghers to make life unpleasant for the robber barons, as early as the 13th century, And this was often more effective in money matters than armed guards.

In 1253, the Westfalian towns of Dortmund, Soest, Munster and Lippstadt entered into an agreement for their mutual defense. The contract contains the following passage: "Whoever shall rob a burgher of these four towns, shall not be assisted by the towns through loans or any other means. The lord of the realm is held responsible for the conduct of his burg wardens and retinue. If any robber is arrested in any one of these four towns, then the plaintiff accusing him shall enjoy the protection of the law in all the other towns, the same as native burghers, The towns protect the lives of all their burghers by giving them armed guards from town to town, A knight who has broken his word, shall be refused credit in all towns, until he shall have met his obligations."

The further development of the credit system and its gradual domination over the monetary system is closely linked with the religious wars of the Reformation. This development is but the reflex of economic transformations, by which the merchant is gradually turned into an industrial capitalist, and by which not only the usurer, but the merchant capitalist himself becomes subject to the sway of the industrial capitalist. And with this dissolution of old economic conditions comes at the same time a dissolution of religious organizations.

"The monetary system is essentially Catholic, the credit-system essentially Protestant. 'The Scotch hate gold'. In the form of paper the monetary existence of commodities has only a social life. It is Faith that makes blessed. Faith in money-value as the immanent spirit of commodities, faith in the prevailing mode of production and its predestined order, faith in the industrial agents of production as mere personifications of self-expanding capital. But the credit system does not emancipate itself from the basis of the monetary system any more than Protestantism emancipates itself from the foundations of Catholicism." (Karl Marx, Capital, Vol III)

The parasitic existence of a ruling class upon the shoulders of a laboring population — that is the historical basis of all money relations as it is of all authoritative creeds. The feudal serfs, and the rising handicrafts men in the towns, these were the productive backbone of feudal society. This society did not fall into the dormant state of Roman civilization because its productive members had from the outset retained some measure of liberty and rights due to their tribal origin. It was this persistent tribal strength which carried them through the entire Middle Ages and gave them power not only to lift ancient slavery into the greater productivity and vitality of feudalism, but also to carry feudalism forward, in spite of the depredations of the feudal lords, the machinations of the financiers, and the bickerings of the merchants, into a system of still higher productive power and still greater possibilities of development, the system of industrial capitalism.

Chapter 12   The Rise Of Industrial Capitalism

The serfs and handicraftsmen of feudal days had one advantage in their struggles against the ruling classes—they were the owners of the essential requirements of production in their respective occupations. The serfs owned the soil which they tilled (originally in communal ownership), the handicraftsmen the tools and materials of their trades. So long as they had this advantage, they could not become the helpless slaves of exploitation.

Originally every feudal commune produced all its own necessities. The members of the *mark* communes produced not merely agricultural crops, but fashioned also the raw materials into finished articles of use. Grain was made into flour, flour into bread; flax was made into yarn, yarn into linen; wood was cut into timber, boards, tool handles, and used in building dwellings, churches, barns, stables. The serfs were farmers, builders, carpenters, joiners, smiths, all in one, and the various members of their families devoted themselves to different trades. Women and children all had to fulfill a useful function in this division of feudal labor.

It was particularly the estates of the feudal lords which afforded the greatest opportunities for the co-operative division of labor, because the lord had the labor-power of the entire commune at his disposal for definite periods of time, and always kept many unfree servants, who had to be maintained by the taxes of the serfs. It was natural that a laborer who had acquired a high skill in some particular craft should be employed as a specialist in that line. In this way the first beginnings of handicrafts were separated from the agricultural pursuits on the feudal estates.

When the town life with its markets developed, and handicrafts found a wider field in this new environment, when the struggle between the merchant class, the future chiefs of industrial capitalism and the feudal nobility waxed fiercer, when the towns became centers of refuge for fugitive serfs, then many of the artisan serfs fled to these havens of peace and assisted the merchants against the feudal barons. From the 11th to the 14th centuries this transfer of handicrafts from the feudal estates to the towns proceeded almost without interruption.

As the population increased and the towns grew, there developed gradually a larger and larger market, not only for the products of industry, but also of agriculture. Since the towns were unable to supply all the needs of their own inhabitants, the farmers were enabled to carry much of their surplus-product to the town markets and thus to secure a thing which they had never handled in old feudal times, namely money.

With the advent of money to the feudal commune and the lord's estate, a new spirit seized the old institutions. So long as the merchant had been the principal owner of money, the feudal barons had secured a part of his wealth by the very simple but effective method of waylaying and robbing him. Since the time of the Crusades, this noble profession of highway robbery had been carried on extensively and it had been the only way to secure money, since the serfs paid their taxes to the lord only in kind.

But when the market expanded and the power of the towns increased, waylaying became more dangerous and less profitable. Often enough the robber baron returned to his castle without the coveted treasures, and with less men and less buoyant body and mind than he sallied forth with. Some never returned at all. Particularly the invention of gunpowder and of guns was a sad blow to the gallant bearers of mailed armor. Knightly warfare became too much like work and lost all the attributes of sport when bullets plunged through the best mailed shirt and iron balls razed the walls of their long impregnable castles. It became necessary to discover an easier and less dangerous, in short a more gentlemanly way of making a living.

Sometimes a gentleman, or a knight, will learn even from a serf and a merchant, particularly if he has to. This is what the chevaliers did when the old method of making money had become obsolete. No sooner did the serfs carry their surplus to the market and bring back to their homes the peaceably secured money of the merchants and other town people, than the knights adopted the same method and prospered. For who was in a better position to throw a large surplus of farm products on the markets than the feudal lord, who had at his beck and call the labor-power of whole communes?

Once the use of money had been established in the hovel and the castle, the idea easily suggested itself to pay the feudal tithes in money instead of in kind. The serfs were in favor of this reform, because they thought it would make them more independent of the lords. The lords liked it, because it offered greater opportunities for securing the luxuries which had become dear to them after they had once been introduced to them by the higher civilization of the Orient. Nor was it long before the lords discovered that it was much easier to squeeze more money out of the serfs than to waylay and rob merchants.

But when the serfs realized that the new reform, instead of freeing them more from their bonds to the lord, was turning into a means of oppressing them harder, they rebelled and fought for a century to escape from this new and more galling bondage. With varying success on both sides, this struggle between serfs and lords, which ran parallel to the struggle between merchants and lords, was carried on, but its final outcome was almost everywhere the gradual emancipation of the serfs from feudal chains.

This compelled the lords to turn to means which should insure a greater productivity of their own estates. At the same time it resulted in the disruption of the old communal fraternity, by allying the well-to-do serfs against their poorer brothers. The more the population increased, the larger became the number of those who were excluded from the old commune and compelled to shift for themselves. Naturally these homeless and landless ones gravitated toward the towns, where they were safe against the attacks of the lords and where the prospects of employment and living were more promising.

Under these circumstances, the lords soon felt the need of productive laborers on their estates. The old armed retinues became a drag on them. Either the warriors had now to exchange the sword for a plow, or they were cast adrift like the surplus population on the farms and compelled to seek new means of livelihood. These new homeless ones, like their fellow serfs, found largely a new home in the towns. But when this tendency became universal, it was not long before a vast multitude of tramps flooded western Europe, in the country districts as well as in the cities. And as the Reformation marched across Europe and disbanded many monasteries, the property owners had to resort to force and coercive laws for the protection of their holdings and wealth.

But do what they might, neither the lords nor the new middle class of the towns could stem the tide of proletarianization. While the middle class itself, at least the rising class of industrial masters, did nothing essentially toward the increase of the proletariat, the lords did so much the more to increase the number of propertyless and homeless wanderers, and to supply the new capitalists with a plentiful harvest of wage workers. The greed for money had seized the nobles, and when their own estates were no longer able to yield all the money needed for their spendthrift habits, they banded together and drove the farmers from their lands and homes.

The increase of the population intensified the sufferings of the homeless ones, and for two centuries, all through the 15th and 16th century, the exodus from the country to the town continued with ever-renewed vigor.

Hardly had the struggle between the middle class and the lords and between the serfs and the lords reached a certain stage of continuity, when a new class struggle arose in the towns themselves. So long as the towns were in need of inhabitants, every productive newcomer had been welcomed and had at once enjoyed all civic rights. But as this movement went its inevitable course, real estate and opportunities in the towns gradually fell into the hands of the elder or economically favored inhabitants, and more and more of the newcomers found themselves without land and without a chance to labor at their trades. The wealthier and established townspeople assumed the role of a privileged class, denied political rights to the new members of the town and proceeded to enforce prerogatives against them in much the same way as the feudal lords had done.

This compelled the unprivileged citizens to organize themselves, in order to secure for themselves the same political rights which the old inhabitants had enjoyed. As early as the 13th century, this new class struggle between town aristocrats and town unprivileged began, and led during the following centuries to the ascendency of the organized crafts, or guilds. At the end of the 15th century, these organizations had succeeded in most towns in securing their political rights.

But in the meantime the population of the towns had continued to increase. A larger and larger number flowed from the country to the town, particularly when the feudal lords began to dispossess the old *mark* communes and to turn the communal lands into sheep walks and deer parks. Already in the beginning of the 16th century most of the large towns counted a vast percentage of paupers among their inhabitants, some of the old chronicles registering as high as 25% of propertyless inside the town walls.

The guilds themselves, instead of enlisting this proletariat in their fight against the town aristocracy, did everything in their power to increase the proletariat, from the moment that its members began to show signs of becoming dangerous competitors of the guild masters. Already in the 14th century we meet in many places with ordinances limiting the number of crafts masters in a certain town, assigning to each master a definite number of journeymen and apprentices, and forbidding competitive crafts of artisans outside of the guilds within a circuit of one mile all about the town.

Under these circumstances, the class struggles between the above mentioned classes were soon accompanied by a new class struggle between journeymen and masters, and by the struggles of the propertyless proletarians against all other classes.

With the beginning of the 16th century, we see everywhere a large class of more or less outlawed proletarians in the principal countries of Europe, wherever the middle class had developed into industrial capitalists and secured a certain degree of importance and recognition in economic and political affairs. This proletariat was not only at the mercy of the feudal and industrial aristocracy, but also despised and shunned by the guilds and the better situated laboring classes. While the guilds, and later the organizations of the journeymen, succeeded here and there in sharing to a moderate extent in the increasing productivity of their labor, the general condition of the laboring classes fell more and more below the level of the average standard of living, which had become established by feudal tradition.

So long as the guildmaster was himself the principal laborer in his shop, employing only a few journeymen and apprentices to assist him, there was little danger of any attempt to prolong the working day beyond reasonable limits. But when the number of journeymen and apprentices increased, when the master was no longer the chief worker but mainly a superintendent, then the struggles between masters and journeymen began to rage about questions of working hours, wages, treatment, etc.

The proletariat, however, unorganized and unprotected, did not and could not take part in these struggles, because the better-situated laboring classes themselves excluded them from all participation in their affairs. It is not strange, therefore, that the protracted struggle between masters and journeymen remained but a sporadic and fierce wrangle between a small number of people, and did not assume the form of a vast labor movement which could become an overwhelming historical force and take part consciously in a transformation of social conditions in harmony with understood historical tendencies. Radical as these journeymen were, their demands never went beyond the ordinary horizon of a willing laborer who is ready to serve his master so long as he is fed and treated well. They had no revolutionary ideal, no wish to abolish master rule in every form.

Like the ruling classes themselves, and like the well-to-do serfs, the guilds had to create the elements of their own downfall by promoting through their anti-progressive actions the formation of a new class of laborers, who should be compelled, through historical necessities, to antagonize not only the guild system and its policies, but the entire social order that had pushed them to the bottom of the social pit. All the classes of feudal society above the proletariat were thus continually engaged in laying the foundation without which no industrial capitalism can exist, a large wage-working proletariat. But of all classes so engaged during this period, the future captains of industry, the merchants, contributed the smallest share toward the creation of their future objects of exploitation.

The historical development set the table for them, as it were, and pushed them into the best seats almost without any exertion of their own. The other classes did most of the work of undermining the old and building up the new system. The most essential part of all this work was the creation of a wage-working proletariat, for without it capitalist industry was impossible.

"The capitalist system presupposes the complete separation of the laborers from all property in the means by which they can realize their labor. As soon as capitalist production is once on its own legs, it not only maintains this separation, but reproduces it on a continually extending scale. The process, therefore, that clears the way for the capitalist system can be none other than the process which takes away from the laborer the possession of his means of production, a process that transforms, on the one hand, the social means of production and subsistence into capital, on the other the immediate producers into wage laborers. The so-called primitive accumulation, therefore, is nothing else than the historical process of divorcing the producer from the means of production. It appears as primitive because it forms the prehistoric stage of capital and of the mode of production corresponding to it. The economic structure of capitalistic society has grown out of the economic structure of feudal society. The dissolution of the latter set free the elements of the former. The immediate producer, the laborer, could only dispose of his own person after he had ceased to be attached to the soil and ceased to be slave, serf, or bondsman of another. To become a free seller of labor-power who carries his commodity wherever he finds a market, he must further have escaped from the regime of the guilds, their rules for apprentices and journeymen, and the impediments of their labor regulations. Hence, the historical movement which changes the producers into wage workers, appears, on the one hand, as their emancipation from serfdom and from the fetters of the guilds, and this side alone exists for our bourgeois historians. But on the other hand, these new freedmen became sellers of themselves only after they had been robbed of all their own means of production, and of all the guarantees of existence afforded by the old feudal arrangements. And the history of this, their expropriation, is written in the annals of mankind in letters of blood and fire. The industrial capitalists, these new potentates, had on their part not only to displace the guildmasters of handicrafts, but also the feudal lords, the possessors of the sources of wealth. In this respect the conquest of social power appears as the fruit of a victorious struggle both against feudal lordship and its revolting prerogative, and against the guilds and the fetters they laid on the free development of production and the free exploitation of man by man." (Karl Marx, Capital, Volume I)

The budding industrial capitalist, then, found an abundance of proletarians at hand. But these proletarians were not trained to suit the requirements of the merchants and financiers, who now started the period of industrial capitalism by the first stages of manufacture. Manufacture was inaugurated in two ways. Either a number of artisans of different trades were employed under the direction of one capitalist in the same workshop, and each contributed his share to the finished product. Or, artisans of the same trade were assembled by one capitalist in one workshop and each artisan fashioned the same article from the first stages to the finished product. This required skilled laborers. But skilled laborers were scarce, and so long as manufacture offered plenty of opportunities for journeymen to become independent masters, the skilled laborers were of an independent turn of mind, resented shop discipline, and gave the capitalists much trouble. The political power of the ruling classes, the state, had to step in and enforce the submission of the laborers to the requirements of capitalist production.

"The proletariat, created by the breaking up of the bands of feudal retainers and by the forcible expropriation of the people from the soil, this 'free' proletariat, could not possibly be absorbed by the nascent manufactures as fast as it was thrown upon the world. On the other hand, these men, suddenly dragged from their wonted mode of life, could not as suddenly adapt themselves to the discipline of their new conditions. They were turned en masse into beggars, robbers, vagabonds—partly from inclination, in most cases from stress of circumstances. Hence at the end of the 15th and during the whole of the 16th century, throughout Western Europe, a bloody legislation against vagabondage. The fathers of the present working class were chastised for their enforced transformation into vagabonds and paupers. Legislation treated them as 'voluntary' criminals, and assumed that it depended on their own good will to go on working under the old conditions that no longer existed." (Karl Marx, Capital, Volume 1)

While the proletariat was thus being prepared for its work under capitalism, the new master class was gradually slipping out of its embryonic form and assuming its typical capitalist character. The expropriation of the serfs from the soil had created the large landed proprietor. Among the serfs which remained on the lord's estates, many developed later into renters and thence into farmers employing wage labor. The great financiers and merchants whom the middle ages had produced, launched out into industrial enterprises as soon as the feudal and corporate barriers that had hedged them in during the old times, fell with the dissolution of the feudal communes and the corporate guilds. Among the former guildmasters, small independent trades people and journeymen, a good many had acquired enough wealth to enable them to hire wage workers and start in capitalist business on their own little scale. And so long as capitalist manufacture absorbed the national industries only by slow and almost imperceptible degrees, the opportunities for the small capitalist were in no danger of being closed by his large competitors.

With the dissolution of the feudal system of production and its patriarchal method of supplying all its wants by home labor, the production of commodities for sale became the predominant mode of supplying the needs of human society. And it was not only the home market which was thus opened for the operations of industrial capital. With the discovery of America, with the opening of the sea routes to India, China, and Japan, by the circumnavigation of Capes Horn and Good Hope, by the discovery of the tropical islands in the Pacific Ocean, vast new foreign markets were unlocked, and the looting of Mexico and Peru by the Spaniards, of East India by the English, of the Malay Archipelago by the Portuguese and Dutch, brought enormous quantities of gold and silver into the hands of the conquerors and dragged a great multitude of cheap laborers from their homes and families, pressing them into the service of industrial capital.

"The discovery of gold and silver in America, the extirpation, enslavement and entombment in mines of the aboriginal population, the beginning of the conquest and looting of the East Indies, the turning of Africa into a warren for the commercial hunting of black skins, signalized the rosy dawn of the era of capitalist production.

"These idyllic proceedings are the chief momenta of primitive accumulation. On their heels treads the commercial war of the European nations, with the globe for a theater. It begins with the revolt of the Netherlands from Spain, assumes giant dimensions in England's anti-Jacobin war, and continues in the opium wars against China, etc. The different moments of primitive accumulation distribute themselves now, more or less in chronological order, particularly over Spain, Portugal, Holland, France and England. In England at the end of the 17th century, they arrive at a systematical combination, embracing the colonies, the national debt, the modern mode of taxation, and the protectionist system. These methods depend in part on brute force, for instance, in the colonial system. But they all enjoy the power of the State, the concentrated and organized force of society, to hasten, hot-house fashion, the process of transformation of the feudal mode of production into the capitalist mode, and to shorten the transition. Force is the midwife of every old society pregnant with a new one. It is itself an economic power." (Karl Marx, Capital, Volume 1). (The passage referring to force as the midwife of old societies pregnant with a new one, and as an economic power, has often been interpreted by anarchists and by bourgeois economists and politicians as an apology of violent measures in the proletarian class struggle against the capitalists. While the historical development does not exclude a cataclysmic development, the above passage refers clearly to the organized force of society as represented by the state, and does not sanction the employment of violent means outside of the organized society. The Marxian conception of history, with its emphatic recognition of the gradual and genetic growth of social transformation, necessarily lays the stress upon the peaceful and legal accomplishment of the proletarian aims, and admits of violent means only as exceptions under particularly abnormal conditions, in which uncontrollable proletarian elements outside of the organized socialist movement rise in spontaneous rebellion against the ruling classes and compel the Socialist Party for the sake of principle to side with the oppressed, as was the case in the Paris Commune. Only after the proletariat has peacefully organized a majority of the voters of a certain country and elected its representatives to the leading public positions, in other words, when the proletariat itself will be the organized power of the state, may force be used "legally" in defense and maintenance of the proletarian position. And in that case the enemies of the proletariat should not complain, for it will then simply be a case of tables turned and of weighing with the same measure.)

In its infancy, the industrial capitalist class found a proletariat ready-made at hand, waiting to be exploited. The old feudal powers in nobility and guilds undermined their own economic foundation and paved the way for the political supremacy of the capitalist class. The working classes fought the battles which secured the political supremacy, or at least a share in it, to the capitalists. In its further growth, many new forces came to the aid of this class, notably steam and its unifying servant, machinery. Soon it was driving along with a speed never before equaled by men, like a new Phaeton driving the horses of the Sun. Like Phaeton too, it is rushing headlong to its doom as no other class before it.

Chapter 13   From Ancient To Classic Economics

Ever since commerce, money, merchants' capital, interest, profit, made their appearance in human society, there have been thinkers who tried to treat of these matters in a scientific way. The first traces of a scientific conception of economic problems, which are known to us by fragments of literature on the subject, are found among the thinkers of ancient Greece, several hundred years before the Christian era.

These men were not brought up in the Mosaic conception that Adam and Eve were thrown out of a paradise and compelled to work for a living after they had made a very natural mistake. Nor were they brought up in the modern conception that capitalists have always existed and will always exist. In fact, they knew that capitalists were a very recent, and by no means welcome, addition to the national life. And they were inclined to regard these newcomers as a nuisance rather than a benefit to society.

In their day, the efforts made by legislators like Solon to protect the property of the mass of the citizens against the greed of merchants and mercantile aristocrats were still vividly remembered. That the private property of a plutocratic minority should be held sacred, and the private property of the vast mass of laboring citizens left at the mercy of a plutocratic minority, did not seem as natural to the public men of Greece as it does to the senators and congressmen of the United States or Rockefeller.

On the other hand, the vast body of laborers in Greece were slaves. Their labor-power and labor-time could not be measured in terms of commerce. Moreover, production was mainly for direct use, and commerce did not reach as deeply into the productive sphere as it did later under different systems of economy.

Under these circumstances, the Grecian economists show neither the exalted reverence of modern partisan economists for the private property of capitalists, nor do they appreciate the vital importance of human labor in the problems of political economy. They deal more with effects than with causes, and puzzle their brains with schemes rather than historical processes. Nevertheless, they make very objective observations and utter many profound ideas, which the partisan economists of modern ruling classes might read with much profit.

Plato, for instance, understood the vital significance of social division of labor for the constitution of the Grecian city. Aristotle realized that commodities have a use-value and an exchange-value. He recognized that money as a medium of circulation performs different functions than money as capital. He even analyzed money as a measure of value, and correctly stated that the value of money must be determined by the same means as that of all other commodities. He was of the opinion that money as a mere medium of circulation owed its existence to agreement or law, that it had no intrinsic value of its own, and that its usefulness as coin was merely an attribute of its function in the circulation. It was evident to him that the exchange-value of commodities was at the bottom of their prices. And since commodities compare their exchange-value only through their prices, he made them measurable through money although he held that the value of the different objects measured by money was really incommensurable. But for all practical purposes he thought that money could be used as a measure of what was in fact not measurable. He was looking for a common unit of measurement. But the basis of Grecian society, slave labor, prevented him very naturally from finding in average social labor time the common measure of all exchange-values.

The Grecian economists went as far as they could under the historical circumstances under which they lived. So long as the social conditions did not offer them the materials necessary for a scientific solution of economic problems, the Grecian thinkers could not well be expected to arrive at a scientific solution.

During the centuries following the dissolution of Grecian societies, the conditions were even less favorable for the development of a science of sociology. Intellectually the Roman civilization never rose to the intensity and perfection of the Grecian. The mental conception of the feudal era, which followed the disintegration of the Roman empire, fell completely into the toils of a mode of thought which turned its eyes inward rather than outward and tried to arrive at objective truths, not by an inductive method of research, collecting and classifying experimental facts and making logical deductions from them, but by shutting out as much as possible of the actual reality and juggling with introspective speculations.

It was only in astronomy, and its auxiliary mathematics, that exact methods of observation and reasoning enforced themselves. And these sciences did not extend their influence into the sphere of social relations.

Wherever we meet with any thought touching upon social matters during the medieval period we find that it is either confined to denunciation of the natural results following from private ownership of land and means of production, with its attending class rule, or to dreamy utopias, passionate revolts, despairing outcries. The oppressed classes lived under conditions which prevented them from developing any consciously organized social movements of such character as would enable them to understand the course of historical evolution and adapt themselves to it as auxiliaries, They generally worked against the prevailing tendencies of social development, not with them. Their revolutions were either short, spasmodic outbreaks, or sentimental and resigned theoretical crusades on the field of abstract ethics.

In short, the requirements for the elaboration of scientific theories did not exist in ancient and medieval societies. Even the best-educated brains of those days were dominated by speculative conceptions, and naturally so. Besides, education was a privilege of the select. Whenever any particularly bright mind showed itself among the oppressed classes, it was generally taken in hand by the ruling classes and educated to serve the interests of caste. If such a man remained loyal to his class he was killed by the rulers. And such loyal leaders of the working class revolution were necessarily as much dominated by speculative fancies as the educated men of the ruling class, for the conceptions of the ruling classes are the prevailing and dominating ones so long as their rule is assured by social evolution.

The first modern attempts to introduce scientific methods into political economy were due to the efforts of the rising merchant towns of Central and Western Europe, from the twelfth to the sixteenth centuries, to overcome the money monopolies of the ruling princes and great financiers. While these efforts were really a struggle of one kind of monopoly against another, their theoretical reflection assumed the guise of a defense of natural laws against feudal laws.

The laws of mercantile economy were defended as "natural" laws against the "unnatural" laws of feudal privilege, for the former were declared to be the expression of "free" competition, while the feudal rights were assailed as artificial gifts of class privilege. This is the historical genesis of the distinction between natural and artificial monopolies, of which some modern would-be economists make so much in their frantic endeavors to defend the little exploiter against the inroads of the large exploiter, and which they proclaim as the theoretical basis of "natural" remedies against industrial and financial trusts.

Out of these first theoretical skirmishes between feudal power and merchants' needs arose the theoretical controversies of the mercantilists against the monetary system that was their mother. In these controversies the superficial notions arising in the brains of the merchants out of the surface indications of commercial processes were pitted against the superstitious speculations of the industrialized champions of feudal privileges, who believed in the immanent mysterious powers of money as the sole source of social wealth. And since money was as much the idol of merchants as of the feudal powers, the entire controversy raged about the peculiar forms and functions of money as a medium of circulation, as a measure of value, as a standard of price, as a hoard, as a means of payment, as interest-bearing and merchants' capital.

The monetary privileges of princes and a few great financiers stood in the way of the merchants. The requirements of extending commerce demanded imperiously a greater flexibility of a circulating medium. This led as early as the twelfth century to the establishment of deposit banks in the Italian merchant towns, and in proportion as the center of commerce was shifted northward and westward in the course of the following centuries, the same institutions appeared among the Dutch and the Hansa towns of Germany.

These deposit banks, in their turn, acquired a monopoly of money, and out of the struggles against bank monopolies arose the credit system, which was in due time to exceed enormously the scope of the precious metals in the circulation of commodities.

This entire controversy about money, dragging its weary length through several centuries, was at first naturally confined to the sphere of circulation. It did not touch the sphere of production because all the essential interests of the contending parties centered around the control of the medium of circulation. That the value of the metal in money itself was not due to any immanent powers of this medium of circulation, but rested in the last analysis upon the productive forces of society, was a conception that did not recommend itself at the outset to the parties most concerned in this controversy. And so the whole theoretical discussion, from the historical point of view, began on a lower level than the speculations of the early Grecian economists. The reason for this state of things is easily found in the historical conditions leading up to these controversies. I need not dwell on this point any further here.

With the further development of the merchant class into a class of industrial capitalists, the sphere of production gradually asserted its influence over the sphere of circulation, and this found expression also in the theoretical discussions. Already in the transition years from the sixteenth to the seventeenth century political economy began to assume its modern aspect and delve into problems of value. In the person of William Petty, the founder of modern political economy, we come face to face with the passage from mercantilist to classic economist theories. He did not only reassert, in a more perfect form, Aristotle's theory of money and of the value of commodities in general, but he even declared definitely that "equal labor" was the common measure of all commodities. But owing to the incompleteness of his theoretical material, and to the undeveloped condition of the working proletariat, he remained in doubt about the practical means by which this common measure could be made serviceable.

Petty's work served as a basis for the entire mercantilist literature during the next century and paved the way for all subsequent analyses of value. His emphasis upon exact methods of observation in sociology by means of statistical tabulation still stands as a lasting rebuke to all modem compilers of official statistics, which seem to be especially designed for the purposes of baffling unbiased sociological research, instead of encouraging and assisting it.

Just as Petty's work represents in England the first systematic theory of mercantilism, so Quesnay's work represents in France the first systematic presentation of capitalist production. Owing to the peculiar historical conditions under which the bourgeois revolution developed and succeeded in France, the physiocratic system of Quesnay considered the capitalist farmers as the typical representatives of industrial capital. For this reason this system remained one-sided and limited in its application. But it brought out at least one very essential point, namely that it is fundamentally not a question of mere production, but of reproduction. In other words, the problem is not merely to explain what capital is, but how it maintains itself intact and increases itself.

The physiocratic character of Quesnay's system made it unintelligible to those economists who developed the theory of industrial capital in England, where industrialism assumed its most typical features. Adam Smith, whose "Wealth of Nations" marks the definite repudiation of mercantilist conceptions in political economy, still gropes his way rather tentatively through the mazes of undifferentiated and undigested thought. He falls in many respects below Quesnay's level, particularly in his analysis of the process of reproduction. But nevertheless he shows his genius by seeking a solution of economic problems above all in the sphere of production, making determined efforts to ascertain the actual relations between labor and capital, and examining the influence of the different component parts of capital on the process of reproduction. Here he is necessarily vague and falls into misleading conceptions, which became pitfalls for the next generation of economists. This greatest error in this respect was that he considered the distinction between fixed and circulating capital, which relates in fact to the different manner in which various parts of capital are circulated, as a fundamental distinction in the process of production. This error barred his way to a solution of the problem of value and surplus-value.

But in spite of this error, the most significant part of his work is the emphasis which he lays upon the problems of value and surplus-value. Already some mercantilists had recognized that the increase of capital must be due to an increase in social values. Where does this increase come from? The greater part of the mercantilists imagined that surplus-value arose from arbitrary additions to the prices of commodities. But even Petty recognized that the surplus-value of the whole society cannot come from mere buying and selling. And Steuart declared frankly that the gains and losses of people cheating one another in buying and selling must mutually balance one another, so that the result is the same as though they had sold their commodities at normal prices. On the other hand, social laws cannot be studied by examining a few exceptions, and so it will not do to explain the origin of the surplus-value of entire classes by occasional gains which a few individuals may realize in commercial competition.

Adam Smith re-asserted the theory of value which was developed in the germ by Petty. In the work of Smith, this theory is made the basis for his analysis of surplus-value. But since he neither perfected Petty's theory of value nor applied it consistently, he got no further than a frank declaration that ground rent and capitalist profit are deductions from the product of productive laborers, who performed surplus-labor over and above the labor required for their own sustenance without receiving an equivalent for it. This did not enable him to discover the mechanism by which particularly the industrial capitalist class secure control of the surplus-products of laborers and realize surplus-value on them in the shape of money. Neither did he separate surplus-value, as a general category, from the different forms which it assumes in industrial profit, merchants' profit, interest on capital, and ground rent.

Adam Smith represents in classic political economy the transition period from manufacture to machinofacture, just as Petty represents theoretically the transition period from mercantilism to manufacture, and Quesnay the transition from agricultural to industrial capitalism.

The next man, who marks in England a new historical stage of production, is David Ricardo, whose most significant work falls into the first quarter of the nineteenth century. He is the typical economist of machine production in industrial capitalism, and, therefore the typical spokesman of bourgeois political economy in its modem form.

Ricardo claimed that the new values added by the labor of the producing workers to the values already incorporated by past labor in raw materials and machinery were divided into capitalist's profits and laborer's wages, and that ground rent was a deduction from the profits of the industrial capitalists. It followed, according to Ricardo, that wages and profit rise and fall in inverse ratio to one another, without directly affecting the general level of prices. So far as prices were subject to fluctuation around the real values of commodities, Ricardo held that these fluctuations were regulated by supply and demand.

All these claims were logical corollaries of his theory of value, and in keeping with his idea that the accumulation of capital and the proportional division of capital into fixed and circulating parts might exercise an influence on the relative values of commodities. But since he made no progress over Adam Smith in this respect, and failed to realize the distinction between the organic composition of capital in the sphere of production and the different ways in which different parts of the value of capitals are circulated, he did not arrive at a consistent scientific solution of the problems of value and surplus-value. Neither did he clearly separate surplus-value as a general category from its particular forms as capitalist profits, landlord's rent, banker's interest. Above all, he failed to draw the logical inferences from his theory of value with regard to the laborer's share in his own product.

But there were others who did. In Ricardo's time the industrial proletariat in England had developed sufficiently to create its own theories, and the spokesmen of this proletariat at once proceeded to combat the capitalist class with the theories of its own thinkers.

Just as Petty's theories had been the pivot around which had turned all mercantilist controversies after him for a century, so Ricardo's theories became the center of more than fifty years of theoretical discussion, and remnants of his theories survived in a more or less muddled form long after the Ricardian school itself had given up the ghost. It was particularly the middle strata of capitalist society who sought consolation in certain portions of Ricardo's theories. Either they clung desperately to Ricardo's theory of value and prayed fervently for system of "free" competition, in which all commodities should be exchanged at their real value without all the other "unnatural" features of capitalist competition which strike such cruel blows at the little exploiter. Or they resurrected a portion of

Ricardo's theory of ground rent and built on it a scheme for the salvation of the middle class. An example of this last method is Henry George's single tax ideas, which are offered to the working class in the hope that it may save the little exploiter from his inevitable fate. The grotesque irony of single tax is that it uses Ricardo's capitalist theory of ground rent as though it were a proletarian theory, that it generalizes Ricardo's economic rent into an indistinct conception of rent comprising many different forms of rent, and that it offers this muddled rehash of a capitalist theory in the interest of the middle class to a working class whose interests demand the abolition of all exploiting classes.

The early champions of the English proletariat paid little heed to such platonic expurgations of Ricardo's theories. They took the bull by the horns and assumed from the very outset an attitude of implacable antagonism to all capitalist forms of exploitation. They met Ricardo's theory of value with the following argument: if labor creates all exchange-values, as you say, then labor should get all it produces. If the exchange-value of a certain product is equal to the labor contained in it and measured by the labor-time consumed in its production, then the exchange-value of one day's labor should be equal to the value of its product. In other words, wages should be equal to the value of the product of labor. But this is not so in reality. It is well known that wages, the value of a definite quantity of labor, are always lower than the value of the product of labor. The socialists invited the capitalists to draw the logical inferences from these facts and stop robbing the laborers. The Ricardian school was unable to solve this puzzle and refute by scientific argument this position of the early socialists. Neither were the early socialists able to prove by what means the mechanism of capitalist production managed to reproduce the capital and profits of the capitalists and the wages of the laborers. A new theory was necessary for the solution of this puzzle. Evidently this could be only a proletarian theory, for the champions of the capitalist class could not well be expected to formulate a theory that would mean the self-destruction of the capitalist class. In short, a new historical class, the proletariat, required a theory of its own, which should represent its own interests and erect its own milestone, just as the preceding stages of capitalist development had each erected its own milestone in economic theories.

This new theory was the crowning work of the life of Karl Marx.

Chapter 14   The Marxian Theory Of Value

The classic bourgeois economists had freed themselves of many of the superficial conceptions which the owners of merchants' capital had handed down to them through the mercantilist theories. Classic bourgeois economy had abandoned the idea of the intrinsic value of money, had realized that the exchange-value of commodities was determined by the quantity of labor realized in them, and had accepted labor instead of money as a measure of exchange-value. But there still remained some mercantilist superstition even in the most advanced minds of the bourgeois economists, and even when they had theoretically repudiated the mercantilist notions, some of these old ideas persistently recurred and marred the clear analysis of men like Adam Smith and Ricardo. One of the most persistent mercantilist notions, which clung very tenaciously to some bourgeois economists, was that supply and demand determined the exchange-value of commodities. Some of the classic bourgeois economists had indeed undertaken to remove the rubbish of this theory of supply and demand, which again and again interfered with the insistent application of the labor theory of value. But in spite of their efforts, this particular mercantilist notion clung grimly to bourgeois economy, and still clings to it to this day.

Marx took up the argument where the advanced classic economists had dropped it. If labor determines the value of commodities, so Marx said, then supply and demand cannot determine it. Labor works its results in the sphere of production. Supply and demand work their results in the sphere of circulation. Evidently the commodities receive their value in the sphere of production, during the labor process. Then supply and demand enter into the problem, when the finished articles are circulated on the market. It is clear, therefore, that supply and demand cannot determine the value of commodities, but at best only modify it. But if supply and demand balance one another, then their influence is nil, and the question still remains, where the value of the commodities comes from in the labor process. Supply and demand must, therefore, be eliminated from the problem of value, until this problem has been solved. What role they play in the sphere of circulation, through which the commodities pass after they have received their value in the sphere of production, remains to be ascertained in its proper place.

In the mercantilist conception, there had been no explanation of the problem, how it is that supply and demand determine prices, when each individual seller is supposed to fix his own prices in order to make profits by selling his articles for more than he paid for them. Still less had there been any explanation of the question, where the additional values which the merchants pocketed came from. In the labor theory of value of the classic economists, this same problem still remained unsolved. They acknowledged that labor created all exchange-values, but they failed to explain how labor did this. Neither had they shown what kind of labor created exchange-value, nor how this labor was to be used as a measure of value, nor how the surplus-value assumed its different forms, nor how value itself was composed out of its different parts. It was not surprising under these circumstances that the inconsistencies of the classic bourgeois economists should become insurmountable obstacles in their attempts to interpret the actual facts of capitalist life.

Marx did not merely restate the classic bourgeois claim that it was the business of scientific explorers to find out what really passed under capitalist production and circulation, and that it was a mistake to use the notions of the human agents in the movements of commodities as a scientific basis. He also carried this idea through to its consistent conclusion and solved the questions which the classic bourgeois economists had left unanswered. The problem was to find out how value was created by human labor, how it was transferred from the different elements of production to the finished articles, how it was modified by competition in the sphere of circulation, and how the human beings who imagined they were fixing prices according to their individual liking were controlled against their will and unconsciously by the mechanical movements of capitalist production and circulation under the influence of the uncontrolled law of value. In other words, the problem was to find out how the mechanical workings of the uncontrolled and little understood laws of the capitalist system enforced themselves against the will and wishes of the human beings who dreamed of being their free makers.

The exchange-value of commodities and labor as a measure of this exchange-value had not been brought into a natural relation with one another by the classic bourgeois economists. In actual life, the exchange-value of commodities expressed itself tangibly in their money-price. This price, and the money-price of labor-power, were not identical. What then was the fundamental relation between money, labor, and the value of the articles produced by labor and circulated by means of money? And what was it that interfered with this relation through the money-price, so that the law of value accomplished its results only through a long succession of irregularities?

Marx answered these questions and thereby opened the secret door which led into the sacred mysteries of capitalist economy.

Capitalist economy, said Marx, places upon the essential elements of social wealth the stamp of commodities, of things made for sale first, for use incidentally. The useful quality of goods, which makes them acceptable to the consumer who buys them, recedes out of sight for the producer who sells them, and yields the place of honor to the money-value which goods represent for the seller. This significant mark of capitalism is forced upon all things which come under its influence.

The most significant commodity on the capitalist market is the labor-power of the wage worker, that is, the brain and muscle power of those who have no other means of existence but the sale of their power, of their own bodies, to some master for a stipulated sum. What the laborer sells to the capitalist is not labor, but the commodity labor-power vested in his body. The laborer's body is the storage tank of his only marketable commodity. This commodity, labor-power, is bought by the capitalist for the purpose of being consumed by him. He buys it at its market-price, as he does all other commodities, and consumes it by putting it to work for his own benefit.

All other commodities are passive during consumption. They are either consumed individually, as are food, clothing, shelter, luxuries, or productively, as are raw materials, machinery, labor-power. When consumed individually, the commodities pass entirely out of existence, and with them passes their value. When consumed productively, their value is transferred to the product into which their substance passes, or in the production of which their own substance wears away.

But labor-power has one quality by which it differs from all other commodities. When it is productively consumed by the capitalist, it does not merely produce other commodities, but it reproduces itself. A part of its product passes into the hands of the capitalist, is taken to the market and sold, and the money received for it is used to buy new raw materials, machinery, labor-power, and to pay the individual expenses of the capitalist. That portion, which is spent for the purchase of labor-power, passes into the hands of the laborer as wages and is used by him for the reproduction and conservation of his labor-power. The laborer buys with his wages necessities of life, builds up new labor-power, and offers it again to the same or to some other capitalist for renewed productive consumption. (In his early works on economics, Marx did not make the distinction between labor and labor-power. In his "Poverty of Philosophy," and his pamphlets on "Wage Labor and Capital" and "'Value, Price and Profit," the term "Labor" still has the same double meaning which it has in the works of the classic bourgeois economists. It may signify labor-power as well as the process of applying it. But in his "Capital," Marx has made this distinction very plain and used it as a basis for his theory of surplus-value.

Let us see, now, how the productive consumption of labor-power in the factory of the capitalist transforms the other elements of production, that is, raw materials, auxiliary materials, and machinery, into commodities and transfers their exchange-values to the finished articles.

All the natural substances which form the bodies of the raw and auxiliary materials and of the machinery, are grown by nature.

Nature creates wealth, but no exchange-values. The exchange-values which natural materials have when they are brought to market, are due to the labor expended in taking them from the place where Nature grew them. Some of the natural materials have been worked up into partly finished articles when they reach the factory. The machinery, likewise, has received its exchange-value through the labor of the people who made it and carried it to the factory and installed it there. All these exchange-values form the constant capital of the capitalist. But this constant capital (raw and auxiliary materials and machinery) is of itself unproductive. It cannot either produce commodities or reproduce itself. It cannot create any new values. It lies unproductive and inert, until the labor-power of the wage laborer touches it with its creative force. In order to secure the use of this labor-power, the capitalist must pay the laborer a certain amount of wages. The money paid out for wages represents the value of the labor-power, in other words, represents the cost of the necessities required to maintain and reproduce the laborer's labor-power under the prevailing conditions of any period of capitalism.

It is only the labor-power of the laborer which represents the productive force of capitalism. It alone can conserve the value of the raw and auxiliary materials and machinery. It alone can create new values. It alone can increase the exchange-value in capitalist society, For this reason Marx calls the money invested in labor-power the "variable capital" of the capitalist.

The laborer applies his labor-power to the raw and auxiliary materials and sets the machinery in motion. While the machinery is running and working on the raw and auxiliary materials under the control of the laborer, it wears away a part of its substance and the value of this worn out portion passes over to the product. In like manner does the value of the raw and auxiliary materials pass over to the product in proportion as these materials are worked up. To the extent that the machinery wears away and the materials are worked up, the value of the constant capital re-appears in the finished product. This is value which already existed before the laborer touched the elements of production. They have simply changed their form. Formerly the values existed in the raw materials and machinery, now they exist in the finished product. But the capitalist does not care merely to reproduce the value of the constant capital. He buys labor-power because he wants to secure new values and increase his capital. These new values are created by the laborer in the labor process. While he works, he adds to the value of the constant capital the value of his wages, which represent the variable capital of the capitalist. In this way, the entire capital of the capitalist (constant and variable) is reproduced by the labor of the laborer. But this would not enable the capitalist to make any profits. If only the capital of the capitalist were continually reproduced, the exchange-value in capitalist society could not increase one whit. Something more must be produced by the laborer while he works, something that existed neither in the value of the constant nor in the value of the variable capital. This new something is "surplus-value". How it is produced we shall see in the next chapter.

The question which interests us at this point is: What kind of labor is it that serves as a universal standard of measurement, and how is it measured?

A farmer's labor is different from a joiner's, a carpenter's from a bricklayer's. How can they be compared in their capacity as creators of exchange-value?

Here Marx makes another step beyond the classic economists. The different kinds of labor as they appear to us in the various professions do not play any role in the formation of exchange-value, any more than the useful substances which induce the buyer to purchase commodities for individual consumption. The labor which is productively consumed and creates exchange-value must be regarded as simple human labor, quite apart from the particular form which it assumes in the various occupations. Simple human labor (labor as a human activity without regard to its particular aim) is the standard by which all kinds of exchange-value are rated.

Does this mean that all labor is rated at the same value, no matter whether it be skilled or unskilled labor? No. It means that all labor producing exchange-value is measured by one and the same labor, and this is human labor considered as a simple human activity regardless of its particular professional form. If complicated, or skilled labor is to be compared with simple labor, it can be done in the same way in which fractions of unequal denominators are compared, that is, the same denominator is used for them all, and then they are compared as fractions with equal denominators. The common denominator of all social labor producing exchange-value is simple human labor. Three hours of simple labor may thus be an equivalent for one hour of complicated labor.

How can simple labor serve as a standard of universal measurement? The time during which it is employed measures it and expresses the social exchange-value of its product. If it takes three hours to make one pair of shoes, then three hours is the value of that pair of 4 shoes. If it takes six hours, then six hours is their exchange-value.

But in that case the product of the slowest or laziest man will be worth more than that of the rapid and industrious worker? It pays to be lazy, then? No, that is not the meaning of the Marxian idea of "exchange-value". There will be more labor expended on the product of the slow worker, but that will not make his product more valuable as a social commodity. From the point of view of human society only that part of a man's labor time counts as marketable exchange-value which is equal to the average time required with the prevailing tools and methods of production for the completion of a certain commodity. If the prevailing mode of making shoes turns out one pair of shoes per hour, while a shoemaker working with obsolete methods requires three hours to make one pair of shoes, then one hour will be the exchange-value of one pair of shoes and the slow shoemaker will have worked two hours for nothing. It is not the individual labor which decides the point. It is the average socially necessary to complete a certain commodity which determines its exchange-value. It is average human labor, considered as simple human labor, and measured by the time socially necessary to complete this particular commodity.

But under capitalism value is not measured by labor. It is measured by money. And the value of the metal in a coin has no genetic relation to the value of the coin as a standard of price, this being fixed by law. This leads the capitalist to imagine that money alone is the real measure of value. He does not understand that the value of the precious metals from which money is coined is itself determined by the quantity of labor required for the production of these metals. If it takes much labor to produce a certain quantity of precious metals, then the value of these metals is high, they are "dear". If it takes little labor to produce these metals, then their value is low, they are "cheap". This law enforces itself upon money, even though legal enactment may decide arbitrarily how much metal a coin shall contain and how much value a coin shall represent.

The universal law of value, then, is this: in proportion as the productivity of labor increases, the commodities produced by it in a certain time carry less labor embodied in themselves. More commodities are produced in the same time, and each commodity represents a smaller quantity of individual value. This must be so, because the same quantity of labor is spread over a larger quantity of commodities.

This general law of value applies to all commodities and asserts itself in spite of the different contending elements that seek to circumvent or overthrow it in capitalist society. It holds good for the commodity labor-power as it does for the commodities gold and silver. By means of it, once that it is understood, all the baffling problems which tantalized the wise men of the bourgeoisie may be traced to their fundamental basis and solved. So long as the movements of the industrial process are little understood and uncontrolled by human beings save for the insignificant and unorganized control of the strongest competitors in the process, the law of value remains the hidden and mysterious power which compels all capitalist agents in the industrial process to conform to its rule on penalty of elimination from the industrial process. Since all the many elements contributing to it are intimately interrelated and act upon one another as cause and effect, the results of this misunderstood and misinterpreted interaction appear to the bourgeois mind as mysteries and are described in obscure and ambiguous language without being clearly explained.

We shall see later how specious and shallow were some of the professional explanations, which were advanced by the bourgeois thinkers under the guise of scientific solutions of economic problems. But before we can discuss these problems intelligently, we must first understand the Marxian theory of surplus-value, which is the inseparable companion of his theory of value.

Chapter 15   The Marxian Theory Of Surplus Value

Under the ancient method of barter, no surplus-value was produced. It is true that one trader could cheat another, or take advantage of his needs to get a larger share of the other's articles than was an equivalent for his own goods. But the total amount of articles produced on either side was not increased by this transaction.

Take it that one trader had 10 head of cattle, another 10 tons of wheat, another 10 casks of wine. If one ton of wheat was the equivalent of one head of cattle, then the possessor of the wheat might be in a position to compel the owner of the cattle, through some stress of circumstances, to give him two head of cattle for one ton of wheat. And if one cask of wine was an equivalent of one ton of wheat, then the owner of the wheat might compel the owner of the wine, under similar conditions of duress, to give him two casks of wine for one ton of wheat. But at the end of this transaction, there would still be ten head of cattle, ten tons of wheat and ten casks of wine, only they would be differently distributed. The total wealth of these three traders would not have increased.

This transaction would only indicate that the value of cattle and of wine had declined compared to the value of wheat. No surplus-value would have been produced. For surplus-value means an addition of new values to already existing ones over and above the cost of the total product to the capitalist class as a whole.

It is also true that the ancient merchants and financiers accumulated wealth by taking unfair advantage of the necessities of others, but even so their transactions did not increase the total wealth of their societies any more than the transactions between those primitive traders did. Such accumulations of wealth could not be accomplished in any other way than by a violation of the law of value. They could not be accomplished by means of it. Under the capitalist system of production, on the other hand, the value regulates the accumulation of surplus-value. The problem is, then, to explain how the capitalist can accumulate surplus-value through the mechanical working of the law of value. Value is produced only in production, and if any surplus-value is accumulated, it must first be produced in the sphere of production. Then it must be taken to the sphere of circulation, to the market, and there it must be realized under conditions of competition, in which the value of commodities and the surplus-value contained in them is modified and differently distributed between the various competitors, but always under the influence of the law of value. It is true that commodities are not sold, as a rule, at their exact labor value. In other words, value and prices are not always identical. But nevertheless, the deviation of the prices of commodities from this value cannot be explained by any other means than by the law of value.

According to the Marxian law of value, labor-power is the only commodity which can reproduce the existing values of a certain society and produce additional values. How does it accomplish that, and how does the capitalist get possession of the additional value?

Since the laborer has no other commodity to sell but his labor-power, and since he cannot employ this labor-power in any other way than by being put to work by the owners of the instruments of production, it follows that he cannot consume his own labor-power, but must submit to having it consumed by the capitalist who employs him. He must sell his labor-power to the capitalist at its average social value, that is, at the value of the necessities of life which are required to maintain and reproduce it. The value of these necessities, in their turn, is determined by the prevailing productivity of the labor employed in their production, and in the production of the machinery and raw materials required in the department of necessities. In other words, the value of the labor-power of the laborers employed in the production of the ordinary necessities of life determines the value of the labor-power of all other laborers. But this must not be understood to signify that the value of labor-power, and the value of labor as an activity producing value, are always identical.

The laborers in the different countries are not living under the same conditions of existence. The standard of living varies in the different countries. Since capitalist production is international, the tendency is to bring the laborers of different countries into competition with one another and to equalize their standard of living as much as possible.

Having bought the labor-power of his employees under these conditions, the capitalist puts it to work in his factory. He compels it to produce useful articles with a view to realizing a profit by the sale of their exchange-values.

Now let us assume that the value of the necessities of life required to maintain the laborer's labor-power for one day and reproduce it for the next day is equivalent to six hours of socially necessary average labor. Let the money-value, or price, of six hours of this labor be $3.00. Then the value of one hour of this labor will be 50 ct.

Our capitalist is a manufacturer of cotton yarn. He must have machinery to spin cotton into yarn. He must buy his raw material, cotton, in the competitive market. He must supply his employees with this machinery and this cotton and set them to work spinning the cotton into yarn.

Let us assume, for the sake of easy figuring, that one pound of cotton makes one pound of yarn, that two pounds of cotton are made into yarn in one hour, and that one spindle is worn out in the manufacture of 100 pounds of yarn, that is, in 50 hours. Let the value of 100 pounds of cotton be $5, equal to 10 hours of average labor socially necessary. Then one pound of cotton will be worth 5 ct., or 6 minutes of such labor. Let the spindles cost $10 each, or 20 hours of such labor.

If 50 hours wear out one spindle, then one hour wears out one fiftieth of a spindle, or 20 cts. worth of spindle.

One hour's spinning turns out two pounds of yarn, hence six hour's spinning will turn out 12 pounds of yarn. What will be the value of these 12 pounds of yarn under these circumstances?

The value of these 12 pounds of yarn will be composed of the value of the worn-out portion of spindle (six times 20 ct., or $1.20), of the value of the worked up cotton (12 pounds, worth 60 ct.), and of the value of the wages of the laborer who spun the cotton into yarn, that is, $3.00. The value of the worn-out spindle and of the cotton, which existed before yarn was spun, has been transferred to the yarn, while the value of the six hours of labor, which are an equivalent for the wages of the spinner (or the variable capital of the capitalist) has been newly added in the labor-process and thus incorporated in the yarn. The total value of these 12 pounds of yarn is, therefore, $1.20 and $0.60 and $3.00 = $4.80. This is exactly the amount which the capitalist has to pay for the production of this yarn. True, he will not pay the laborer his $3.00 until the yarn is produced, and in so far the laborer advances to the capitalist the wages which he will receive. But at any rate, the capitalist must pay these $3.00, and after he has paid them, he has no more value in his hands in the shape of yarn than he had when this value existed in the spindles, in the cotton, and in the labor-power of a the spinner. The capitalist cannot make any profits in this way. For according to our theory of value, the surplus-value which the capitalist pockets as his profits under the capitalist system of production, aside from irregularities which violate the law of value, must come from new values which are added by the labor of the productive laborers to the already existing ones. It is indeed true that such profits as were made under the primitive modes of barter by cheating or taking advantage of the unfortunate situations of others, may still be made under the capitalist mode of production. But all capitalists cannot make profits by cheating one another, and such profits are not surplus-value as understood in the Marxian theory. The profits from surplus-value must therefore be explained in some other way. Since there is no surplus-value in these 12 pounds of yarn, the capitalist cannot realize any profit on it, although he may be able to sell this yarn above its value and thus cheat some customer. But this is not capitalist profit as we understand it here, because cheating does not add any new values to the total values existing. If our capitalist wants to make such profits as we have in mind here, he must secure some yarn which costs him nothing for labor. How can he accomplish this?

Our capitalist is not worrying. He has bought the labor-power of his spinner at a price which is equal to 6 hours of socially necessary labor. The spinner has worked six hours and reproduced the outlay of the capitalist for machinery and raw materials used up in the manufacture of the yarn. He has furthermore produced his own wages and added their value to the yarn. He has performed labor equivalent to the price of his labor-power. Does the capitalist now pay the spinner off and dismiss him? By no means. The working day in our capitalist's factory has 12 working hours. The spinner must work six hours longer. In these additional six hours he spins up 12 pounds of cotton more into 12 pounds of yarn and wears out another $1.20 worth of spindle. At the end of 12 hours, the spinner has produced 24 pounds of yam.

What is the value of these 24 pounds of yarn? Evidently it is composed of $2.40 for wear and tear of the spindle, $1.20 for cotton, and $6.00 as an equivalent for 12 hours of socially necessary average labor. The total value of these 24 pounds of yarn is therefore $9.60.

But how much does the production of these 24 pounds of yarn cost our capitalist? He has paid $ 2.40 for cotton, (provided he did not get these things on credit). He will have to pay the spinner $3.00 in wages (unless he compels him to yield up a part of his wages as fines).

At the worst the total cost of these 24 pounds of cotton to the capitalist will be $6.60. The laborer has worked six hours for nothing and the capitalist pockets $3.00 of surplus-value (the value of six hours of surplus-labor) and calls it his "profit", which he has "earned" by his superior ability and enterprise. He has consumed the labor-power of the spinner six hours longer than he has paid for it. And even before he pays the spinner for the other six hours, the spinner has left in the hands of the capitalist the value of his wages in the shape of cotton. It is true the capitalist may have to pay the spinner's wages before this cotton is sold. But at any rate, whether the capitalist sells now or later, he has the value of the money which he pays for wages in his hands and will recover the money when he sells his yarn (irregularities always excepted). Nevertheless, Mr. Capitalist flatters himself that he is keeping the laborer alive by giving him work, and is highly indignant if the laborer refuses to see that the working people would starve to death if the capitalist did not employ and rob them.

Of course, we do not intend to deny that some capitalists may also work, yes, that some of them may even work longer than is necessary to pay for the reproduction of their labor-power. To the extent that they do so, they are producers of their own surplus-value. But in so far as they employ the labor of wage laborers at the same time, they are capitalists and pocket the value of the unpaid surplus-labor of their employees.

We have seen that the value of the individual commodities decreases in proportion as the productivity of labor increases, because more commodities are then produced in the same time and each commodity contains less labor and, therefore, less value. In the same way, the amount of surplus-value contained in every individual commodity decreases in proportion as the productivity of labor increases, because each commodity then contains less surplus-labor.

The productivity of labor never increases simultaneously in the same proportion in all spheres of production. For this reason, it is important to understand the bearing of the distinction between the mere transfer of old values (in machinery and raw materials) to the product, and the creation of new values by the labor process. Of course, both the old and the new values are transferred or incorporated in the product. But whereas the old values are merely transferred from the machinery and raw materials to the finished product, the new values (variable capital and surplus-value) are transferred while in process of creation. It makes a difference in the value of the product whether the productivity of labor increases in the spheres where raw materials and machinery are produced, or in the sphere where the finished article is made, or in the sphere where the necessities of life are made which constitute an equivalent for the laborer's wages. If the productivity increases in the spheres where raw materials and machinery are made, while it remains the same in spheres where the finished article and the necessities of life are created, then less constant value is transferred to the finished article (cotton yarn), but the same quantity of yarn will be turned out in the same time. The total product will have less value, but the surplus-value will remain the same, so long as the hours of surplus-labor remain unchanged. If the productivity of labor increases in the manufacture of cotton yarn while it remains unchanged in the departments of machinery, raw materials, and necessities, then more constant value will be transferred to the product in the same time, because more cotton will be worked up and more spindles worn out. The total product will have more value, but the necessary and surplus-labor-time will remain the same, the same variable capital and the same surplus-value will be newly produced. For so long as the proportion between necessary and surplus-labor is not changed, the amount of variable capital and surplus-value will remain the same.

It is understood, of course, that the value of one hour of socially necessary average labor (50ct according to our example) will remain unaltered, even though the value of labor-power should vary. For if the value of the labor should fall in proportion as that of labor-power falls, then the ratio between necessary and surplus-labor would not be altered by such a variation in value and the production of surplus-value would not be increased. We will not investigate at this point how it is possible that the value of the average labor socially necessary to produce a certain commodity can remain the same when the value of the labor-power, and thus of the necessary labor required to reproduce it, varies. It is enough to point out that this is the assumption on which Marx proceeds in his theory of surplus-value, and the reader must look for a detailed investigation of this point in Marx's work.

Let one working hour (socially necessary average labor) be worth 50ct, as before. Now let the productivity of labor in the department of necessities, and in the departments producing machinery and raw materials for the department of necessities, be doubled. Then the value of necessities, according to the Marxian theory of value, will fall by one half, because twice the quantity of commodities is produced in the same time. If this lasts permanently or continues in the same direction, then the value of labor- power in general will follow the value of necessities. Formerly it required $3 worth of necessities, or six hours of socially necessary average labor, to reproduce the labor-power of the laborers working in the manufacture of cotton yarn. Now the same quantity of necessities can be bought for $1.50, the equivalent of 3 hours of social necessary average labor. Therefore it will require only three hours of necessary labor in the manufacture of cotton yarn to produce the variable capital, and nine hours instead of six will be surplus-labor, so that the surplus-value will be $4.50 instead of $3.00. But the total value of the product, 24 pounds of yarn, will be the same, as the following figures will show (assuming that the productivity of labor in all other departments has remained the same): wear and tear of spindle $2.40; cotton $1.20; necessary labor $1.50; surplus-labor $4.50; total value $9.60. Cost to the capitalist $5.10. Surplus-Value $4.50.

On the other hand, if the value of the socially necessary average labor should fall everywhere in proportion with the fall in the value of labor-power, then we should get the following result: value of labor-power fallen by one half, in other words, value $1.50 instead of $3.00. Value of labor fallen by one half, in other words, one hour of socially necessary average labor worth 25c instead of 50c. Value of product: wear and tear of spindle $1.20; cotton $0.60; necessary labor, 6 hours, or $1.50; surplus-labor, six hours, or $1.50; total value $4.80; surplus-value $1.50. All prices (or values) would have fallen by one half in the whole society, and the result for the surplus-value of the capitalist would be the same as though no change had taken place at all because all values will then be reduced by one half. The Marxian theory of surplus-value necessarily and logically goes on the assumption that the value of the socially necessary average labor in the various departments does not simultaneously follow the variations in the value of labor-power, due to the change of productivity in the department of necessities (and the departments supplying this department with machinery and raw materials).

"In order to effect a fall in the value of labor-power, the increase in the productiveness of labor must seize those branches of industry whose products determine the value of labor-power, and consequently belong to the class of customary means of subsistence, or are capable of supplying the place of those means. But the value of a commodity is determined not only by the quantity of labor which the laborer directly bestows upon that commodity, but also by the labor contained in the means of production. For instance, the value of a pair of boots depends not only on the cobbler's labor, but also on the value of the leather, wax, thread, etc. Hence, a fall in the value of labor-power is also brought about by an increase in the productiveness of labor, and by a corresponding cheapening of commodities in those industries which supply the instruments of labor and the raw material that form the material elements of the constant capital required for producing the necessaries of life. But an increase in the productiveness of labor in those branches of industry which supply neither the necessaries of life, nor the means of production for such necessaries, leaves the value of labor-power undisturbed." (Karl Marx, Capital, Volume 1) Another method of increasing the surplus-labor and reducing the necessary labor is that of intensifying the exploitation of labor. This means that more labor is performed, and the more value created, in the same time or in less time, whereby the variable capital is produced in a shorter time and more surplus-value created without a prolongation of the working day. Intensity of labor increases the value of the product, whereas productivity of labor permits of the production of a larger product with less value in the same or n shorter time.

It follows from the above that the most significant activity of labor-power under capitalism is not the transfer of the value of constant elements of production to the finished product, but rather the creation of new values (variable capital and surplus-value), and that only those changes in the productivity of labor have any direct influence upon the production of surplus-value which change the value of labor-power and at the same time the proportion of necessary to surplus-labor.

The value of labor-power cannot be changed in any other way than by altering the value of the necessities, and the proportion between necessary and surplus-labor can be changed (to the advantage of the capitalist) only by a prolongation of the working day beyond the average, so that the hours of surplus-labor will be increased, or by a reduction of the necessary labor compared to the surplus-labor while the working day remains unchanged.

Marx calls surplus-value produced by a prolongation of the working day beyond the average length "absolute surplus-value". Surplus-value produced by an increase of the surplus-labor within limits of the average working day, that is, by a relative reduction of the necessary labor, is "relative surplus value". The production of relative surplus-value is the typical method of increasing the profits of the capitalist under industrial capitalism. What role this method plays specifically in the era of modern machine production, we shall see in another place.

Chapter 16   Merchants' Capital Under Capitalism

After the commodities have been produced in the sphere of production and charged with a certain amount of value and surplus-value, they must be taken to the sphere of circulation and sold in order that the value of the constant and variable capital may be recovered and the surplus-value in the commodities realized by their sale. The complete cycle of the total capital from the time of its entry into the process of production until the time of its return from the sphere of circulation to its point of departure is called the "turn-over" of capital. But each turn-over must bring back a certain amount of surplus-value, otherwise the process of rotation from the sphere of production via the sphere of circulation and back to the point of beginning has been in vain from the point of view of the capitalist. For the entire capitalist process is not merely a process of reproduction of invested capital, but a process of reproduction on an enlarged scale. The scale of production cannot be enlarged without the investment of some surplus-value. This enlarging of the scale of production is not due to the mere personal desire of the capitalist to realize more profits by the creation of more surplus-value, but an inevitable necessity under the lash of competition, which gives the palm of victory to those whose capitals are best organized to increase the productivity of the labor in their department, to reduce the value of their commodities by this means and thus be able to undersell their competitors and still make the same or a greater profit than they. Only by this means is it possible, at the same time, to reduce the number of laborers and thus the amount of variable capital in proportion to the constant capital and still produce as many or more commodities than with a greater number of laborers under the less-productive methods.

But the turn-over of capital does not proceed as uniformly as the capitalist might wish. All the different parts of which the value of a commodity is composed do not circulate together, nor do they return together to their point of departure. For instance, the whole constant capital is not turned over together, nor do the different elements of the constant capital circulate in the same way. Neither does the variable capital circulate in the same way as certain parts of the constant capital.

Let us take a closer look at the different elements of value, for instance the different elements of which the value of our 24 pounds of cotton yarn is composed. We have seen that 24 pounds of cotton yarn, produced in 12 hours of average social labor, at 50c per hour, had a value of $9.60 to wit, $2.40 wear and tear of a spindle, $1.20 cotton, and $6.00 labor (including $3.00 surplus-labor). The value of the whole spindle, or $10, is not transferred entirely to these 24 pounds of cotton yarn. Only $2.40 worth of spindle are transferred. On the other hand, the value of the 24 pounds of cotton, which are made into 24 pounds of yarn, is entirely transferred to the yarn. The value of labor-power (or of the variable capital of the capitalist) is likewise transferred entirely to these 24 pounds of cotton yarn. But the capitalist cannot buy a spindle piecemeal unless he gets it on credit or pays for it on the installment plan. He must pay for the whole spindle when he buys it. The whole spindle performs its service in the manufacture of 24 pounds of cotton, but only twelve fiftieths of the spindle are worn away in this work, and only that much of its exchange-value transferred to this yarn. The capitalist cannot recover the entire value of this spindle by selling these 24 pounds of yarn. He will have to sell 100 pounds of yarn before he can recover the entire value of his spindle.

What happens here on a small scale happens on a large scale in every great industrial establishment. Large sums of money are tied up in machinery, and are recovered only by degrees as the process of turn-over goes on. But if the capitalist desires to make profits without interruption, he must keep the process of reproduction running without interruption. And if he must pay out large sums of money in one bulk for machinery, but can recover this money only piecemeal after a long period of time, then he must have money in reserve in order to buy more machinery for the expansion of his business, before he has recovered the full amount invested in the old machinery.

This difference in the turn-over in the various elements of a commodity's value plays a significant role in capitalist competition, as we shall see later. Marx calls the capital invested in machinery and circulated piecemeal "fixed constant capital", and the constant capital invested in raw materials, etc., and circulated all at one time "circulating constant capital". The variable capital is likewise recovered in full by the sale of the commodities containing its value, and is to that extent a circulating capital in the same class with the circulating constant capital.

Since a commodity is not produced from the point of view of the capitalist until he has sold it and received its value in money, the circulation of commodities is a necessary and important part of capitalist activity. The quicker the capitalist can sell his commodities, the sooner will he reproduce his capital and pocket his profits. But the selling of commodities requires time and expenses. If the manufacturing capitalist wants to be his own merchant and sell his own commodities, he must have a special department in his establishment attending to the sales. For this purpose, he must invest a large portion of his capital unproductively and tie it up in the sales department. Whatever he has tied up in this fashion, he cannot invest as productive capital. It will not produce any surplus-value. It is a dead expense to him. The labor of the wage workers in the sales department is also unproductive from the point of view of society, because it does not produce any new values but only assists in the circulation of already existing values. Of course, the labor of these wage workers is socially necessary, because the product must be sold before the capitalist can recover its value. But it is unproductive labor and belongs to the dead expense of social production. So far as the relation of these wage workers to the capitalist is concerned, he pays them only for their labor-power, not for the time that he employs them, just as he does with the productive laborers who create value and surplus-value. To that extent, the wage workers in the department of circulation are exploited like the wage workers in the department of production. But they do not produce any surplus-value for the capitalist. They merely save some of the already produced surplus-value for him in proportion as they work longer than they are paid for and thus sell more commodities and help to realize more of the already existing surplus-value for him than he could realize if they worked shorter hours.

We see, then, that every industrial capitalist must have, not merely a certain amount of money with which to buy machinery, raw materials, and labor-power for productive consumption and the creation of surplus-value, but also a reserve fund of money with which to keep the turn-over of his capital in regular flow at points where it would otherwise stop on account of the different modes of circulation of the various parts of constant and variable capital. He must, furthermore, have a reserve fund of money with which to maintain a sales department, if he wishes to be his own merchant.

One of the dearest wishes of the capitalist is to turn his capital over as fast as possible, or, as he puts it, to get quick returns on his money. But under capitalism, things do not always run smoothly. Everything does not go to the liking of the capitalist. Where so many divergent interests are continually battling for supremacy, and where each one takes only his own interests into account regardless of the injury he may inflict upon others and upon the whole social process, the capitalist often finds himself thwarted by forces stronger than he, and the whole capitalist class meets occasionally with disaster due to the heedless manner of its business administration. Commodities do not always sell as easily as the capitalist would wish, money is not always ready at hand for running expenses, and again and again the entire process threatens to come to a standstill and wreck the plans of the profit-hunter.

So we find him continually scheming to circumvent the inexorable laws of capitalist production, which he cannot control, and to turn his capital over quickly by means, which give him temporary relief without a guarantee of success in the end.

One way of getting rid quickly of his newly produced commodities is to sell them to somebody who will undertake the risk of mere buying and selling, without going into the sphere of production. In this way, a division of labor arises between the industrial capitalist, who confines himself to the sphere of production, and the merchant capitalist, who operates wholly in the sphere of circulation. Since the turn-over of industrial capital comprises the entire process of its reproduction, that is, both production and circulation, the easiest way of escaping the vicissitudes of the circulation is to let somebody else worry about them. But it is evident that the merchant capitalist, who undertakes the risk of circulating the products of the industrial capitalist, will not do so for pleasure, but will exact a certain reward from the industrial capitalist for his risk. In other words, the industrial capitalist must sell his commodities to the merchant capitalist at a lower figure than he would ask if he sold them himself. He must yield up a portion of his profits to the merchant.

In the minds of the merchant and the industrial capitalist, however, this transaction does not appear in this light. The industrial capitalist thinks rather that he is adding his profit to his cost-price, and the merchant thinks he is adding his profit to the price which he paid to the industrial capitalist. But the law of value teaches us that this is not the actual condition of things.

"The capitalist must indeed 'sell dearer than he has bought', but he succeeds in doing so only because the capitalist process of production enables him to transform the cheaper commodity which contains less value, into a dearer commodity with increased value. He sells dearer, not because he gets more than the value of his commodity, but because his commodity contains a greater value than that contained in the natural elements of its production." (Karl Marx, Capital. Volume. II) In volumes I and II of his work, and in the first seven chapters of volume III, Marx assumed for the sake of simplicity that all commodities were sold at their average social value, because the irregularities and deviations of price from value in the sphere of circulation could not be clearly explained until he had analyzed how things went when everything passed off regularly. But his theory of value, when applied to the actual conditions of capitalist society, explains in fact how it is that commodities are, as a rule, not sold at their values. Many of the younger students of Marx, particularly in the United States (and none more so than the theoretical thinkers of the Socialist Labor Party who claim to be the only true Marxians) have interpreted the Marxian theory of value in the purely theoretical sense in which it was tentatively developed by Marx as an introduction to a practical application of his theoretical findings in volume III of his work. These misinterpreters of Marx have assumed that the law of value operates with the exactness of a mathematical law. A careful reading even of volume I of Marx's main work should have sufficed to prevent such a rigid interpretation of the law of value.

In other words, this is the actual state of affairs in the transaction between industrial capitalists and capitalist merchants: the wage laborers of the industrial capitalist have produced a certain product, let us say cotton yarn. According to our example, 24 pounds of cotton yarn have a value of $9.60, of which $3.00 are surplus-value. In that case, 2,400 pounds of cotton yarn will have a value of $960, of which $300 are surplus-value. If the industrial capitalist were to attempt to be his own merchant, he would have to invest a certain amount of money in a sales department, and would have to wait for the return of his productively invested money (with a surplus-value) until he could sell the whole 2,400 pounds of cotton yarn. In that case, he would have to invest some reserve funds unproductively in a sales department and productively in the industrial department in order to keep his production running uninterruptedly, even on the same scale. But now suppose some merchant capitalist offers to buy the whole output of 2,400 pounds of yarn in bulk. Of course this merchant wants to make a profit on this transaction. Aside from irregularities which may enable him to make a profit even if he bought this yarn at its full value of $960, he cannot make any profits unless the industrial capitalist sells him this yarn below its value and thus yields up a portion of the surplus-value contained in it. On the other hand, the industrial capitalist would not consent to giving up a portion of his surplus-value unless he would lose less productive capital thereby than he would by being his own merchant and investing some unproductive capital himself. This unproductive capital is now invested by the merchant. The capital of the merchant cannot produce any surplus-value of itself by mere buying and selling, although it may secure some extra profit by irregularities. The transfer of the commercial function from the industrial capitalist to the merchant cannot make this unproductive function productive. Hence the industrial capitalist consents to selling his yarn below its value, say at $810, yielding $150 of his $300 of surplus-value to the merchant. These $810 pay the industrial capitalist for his constant and variable capital ($660) and leave him a surplus-value of $150, a part of which he uses for the enlargement of his scale of production by buying with it more spindles, cotton, and labor-power, and the rest of which he spends for his own individual expenses. He can much better afford to yield up a portion of his surplus-value for the sake of recovering his productive capital quickly, than to invest a large amount of money unproductively in a sales department which would permanently swallow a much larger share of surplus-value.

On the other hand, the capitalist merchant has now commodities valued at $960, of which $150 represent surplus-value pocketed by the industrial capitalist and paid by the merchant, and $150 represent surplus-value yielded up by the industrial capitalist to the merchant and to be realized by the sale of the yarn. The merchant has invested a certain amount of money capital in a store, equipment, and wage laborers (clerks, salesmen, etc.). These wage laborers are unproductive like the merchant himself although they work for him a longer time than he pays for. But their surplus-labor is as unproductive as the capital of the merchant. They merely realize the surplus-value for the merchant which was produced in the sphere of production, and make profits for him so much quicker the more their unproductive surplus-labor is extended and their necessary labor shortened.

If the merchant now sells the yarn at its value, he realizes the surplus-value of $150 and pockets it as his profit. If he does not sell the yarn at its value, but makes an extra profit by selling it above its value, then the extra money which he gets, say, from some wage worker, is not an additional value produced by society, but merely a larger portion taken out of the wages of this laborer, and these wages represent but a part of the variable capital of the industrial capitalist who employed him. From the point of view of capitalist production, this extra profit of the merchant is not additional surplus-value. But from the point of view of the laborer it is additional exploitation, because he could have bought more for the same money had the merchant sold the yarn at its value.

Looking at the question of extra profit in the circulation from the standpoint of the economist who views the social process in its entirety, we can say with Marx: "If the commodities are sold at their values, then the magnitude in the hands of the buyer and seller remains unchanged. Only the form of its existence is changed. If the commodities are not sold at their value, then the sum of the converted values remains the same; the plus on one side is offset by a minus in the other." (Karl Marx, Capital, Volume II)

But it is evident, from the individual laborer's point of view, that he receives a smaller quantity of use-value and exchange-value when he pays more than the value of the yarn to the merchant, or buys shoddy under the impression that he is buying genuine cotton yarn. And in that case, the above passage from Marx cannot mean anything else but that the plus on the side of the merchant is offset by a minus on the part of the laborer.

We have already seen that the merchant's function, while unproductive, is socially necessary, because the process of reproduction includes and requires such an unproductive function. The same is true of the agent entrusted by the industrial capitalist with this function, or of the wage laborer, who perform the laboring part of this function for the merchant. They belong all of them to the unproductive expenses of the social labor process. They perform this unproductive task as a part of the social division of labor, but a division of labor cannot transform a previously unproductive function into a productive one by a mere transfer of this function from one to another. All expenses of circulation which are due to the mere change of form, that is, which merely transfer values from one hand to another or one form to another, do not add any value to the commodities, even though such expenses are socially necessary.

But not all expenses of circulation are of this kind. There are certain expenses of circulation which "may arise from processes of production, which are continued in circulation, the productive character of which is merely concealed by the form of the circulation. Or, on the other hand, they may represent, from the standpoint of society, mere unproductive expenses of subjective or materialized labor, while for this very reason they may become productive of value for the individual capitalist, by making an addition to the price of his commodities." (Karl Marx, Capital, Volume II)

This means that certain expenses may be dead expenses from the point of view of society, but may require additional labor for which the capitalist has to pay, and this extra expense is added by him to the price of commodities and becomes a source of profit for him, to the extent that the unproductive laborers perform surplus-labor. The money for this extra profit comes out of the pockets of the buyers and represents a deduction from their earnings.

Among the expenses of this class are those for storage and the formation of a normal supply of commodities large enough to keep the process of reproduction in uninterrupted flow. These expenses require the investment of unproductive capital, and are to that extent deductions from the productive capital of society. But for the individual capitalist they represent additions to the price of his commodities, and since all labor which adds value also adds surplus-value, the capitalist may increase his profits through such labor, unproductive though it be from the point of view of society. But the rule is that so long as such expenses are socially necessary to keep the process of reproduction going, the capitalist can add them to the price of his commodities. But if they are expenses for more than the necessary supply of commodities under prevailing conditions of reproduction, the best and latest commodities take precedence over the older and poorer ones in the competitive struggle, and the capitalists with excessive expenses of circulation lose that much, because competition does not permit them to add more than the average to their prices for expenses.

Among the expenses which appear on the surface as mere expenses of circulation, but are in fact additions of value to the product, are the expenses of transportation.

Marx classes the transportation industry as a connecting link between the sphere of production and circulation, and calls the capital invested in transportation "productive capital".

The expenses of circulation are not the only unproductive expenditures of capitalist society. Merchants' capital is not merely commercial capital but also financial capital, that is, money used as a means of accumulating surplus-value without taking any actual part either in the production or circulation of commodities in the hands of the person who owns it.

The industrial capitalist may need money before he can recover his capital and reinvest it, or before he can realize all the surplus-value in his commodities and use it to enlarge the scale of his production. He may want to invest more capital before his own business has produced it, on the assumption that he could make more profits if he had more capital right away instead of waiting for it several months or longer. In that case he must borrow money from those who make it their business to hoard it and lend it out at interest. Under the capitalist mode of production this business is overwhelmingly in the hands of bankers. If a man has $100, which he does not care to invest himself, but is willing to lend to someone who will invest it in a productive enterprise, he practically holds in his hands a potential productive capital. If this enterprising man is willing to pay to the owner of the $100 a part of the surplus-value which he will produce by means of this sum, he pays for the use-value which these $100 have in productive enterprise. The amount paid by the user of borrowed money to its owner is called "interest", and comes, like the profit of the merchant, out of the surplus-values produced by the productive laborers.

Marx calls the profits which remain after the deduction of the interest, "profits of enterprise".

Under all circumstances both commercial and financial capital (or, generally speaking, merchants' capital) do not dominate the sphere of circulation any more as soon as industrial capital has become lord of production. Under the precapitalist modes of production, merchants' capital was lord in the sphere of circulation and invaded and corroded even the sphere of production. But when industrial capital has once captured the sphere of production, its turn-overs dominate also the turn-overs of all capitals invested in the sphere of circulation. Capitalist production thus subjects merchants' capital to the requirements of industrial capital, so that, in the last analysis, the merchants' profits as well as the bankers' interest are determined by the rate of profits harvested by the industrial capitalist. And only when the profits of the industrial capitalist are explained can the source and fluctuations of the merchants' profit and the bankers' interest be explained and their role in the turn-over of industrial capital understood.

Chapter 17   Ground Rent

Private ownership of land, like private ownership of capital, has gone through many different forms. Before we discuss the peculiar form of ground rent which is typical of the capitalist system of production, we will take a short glance at other forms which preceded it in the historical order.

In ancient and medieval times, ground rent was paid in kind, that is, in labor, products of the soil, or cattle, not in money. Capitalist renters of the modern kind, that is, farmers investing capital in rented land and exploiting wage laborers on this land, did not exist in ancient or medieval time. Only in ancient Rome and Carthage, at a certain period of their most developed form, did large contractors rent land from the state and till this land by the help of paid laborers with a view to exporting their products. But these were rare and passing exceptions. Rent as a specific kind of surplus-value, as a surplus exceeding the average capitalist profit and drawn by the owner of the soil out of the pockets of the productive capitalist, did not come into existence as the prevalent form until industrial capital became dominant.

The simplest and most primitive form of rent, which has persisted by the side of other forms of rent to this day, is rent paid in the form of labor. The privilege of tilling a certain piece of land is granted on condition that the laborer perform a certain amount of labor on the land of the owner. This kind of rent is still prevalent in a vast portion of the Southern states of North America.

This was the typical form of rent in feudal times. The serf worked with his implements and animals so many days on the estate of the feudal lord, without receiving any equivalent in return for this labor. The remainder of the week the serf worked on his own land. Under such a system, rent and surplus-value are identical. The serf knows exactly how much surplus-labor he performs without an equivalent.

If this labor rent is transformed into produce rent, it does not alter its economic character. Rent in kind, even when it has become the predominant form, is still a modified sort of labor rent, and often accompanied by direct survivals of labor rent, for instance, by forced labor for the lord or the state.

Rent in kind is not paid by performing surplus-labor on the land of the lord but on the serf's own land and delivering the surplus-product of his land to the lord. This form of rent, like the more primitive ones preceding it and persisting by its side, is based on a mode of production which combines agricultural and industrial family labor, and rent in kind is paid in both agricultural and industrial products.

Under labor rent as well as under rent in kind, particularly under the latter (as the predominating form of rent), the laborer may accumulate considerable wealth for himself, and may even rise to a point which permits him to exploit other laborers working under his supervision. This mode of production, resting on a technical basis which does not offer any great opportunities for deep-reaching changes of methods, is very stable and may become almost stationary, as it has in Asia for thousands of years. If a ruling class from a more advanced system of production, for instance of a commercial nation, invades such a system of rent in kind and seeks to exploit it for the purposes of commerce, this form of rent may be carried to such extremes that even the requirements of reproduction (sufficient seeds, cattle, crop rotation, systematic tillage) are endangered and millions exposed to periodical cycles of starvation. See, for instance, British East India.

Rent in kind lends itself most easily to a transformation of rent in money, the form next in the historical order. Money rent is conditioned on a considerable development of commerce, city industries, production for exchange rather than use in general. This implies a general circulation of money as the typical medium of exchange. It implies that markets have become established in which the average prices of commodities approach their social values, a thing which is not necessarily the case in preceding stages.

Money rent is a modified form of rent in kind. The producer pays to the landlord the money-price of the produce instead of the produce itself. In other words, the producer must sell his products in the market, and deliver the money for his surplus-product to the landlord. The tendency to bring this kind of rent into vogue indicates that feudalism is in the stage of transition to modern capitalism, that feudal production is losing its self-supporting character, and that the requirements of commerce compel the feudal classes to get in touch with the new rising strata of society.

This is the stage of the Wat Tyler rebellion, and its theoretical reflection brings forth such vague speculations as Wickliff's "theory of dominion", while the poetical reflex of the struggles and longings of the peasantry and small burghers is found in such dreamy appeals to individual righteousness as Langland's "Vision Concerning Piers the Plowman." At a more advanced stage of this form of rent, when its capitalist character has asserted itself and turned from a revolutionary ideal into a practical method of transforming farmers into debtors, centralizing money into the hands of bankers, and figuring interest at a compound rate, the dreamy poetry gives way to fierce denunciation and the sober reality dispels the "visions" and stalks with bloody heels through the wars of the Reformation.

Money rent is the last of the historical forms of ground rent in which rent absorbs all the surplus- value of production. In its further development, money rent leads to the transfer of the land to the free ownership of the peasant, and to his exploitation by means of capitalist commerce, or else to the capitalist form of ground rent, that is, rent paid by a capitalist farmer to the owner of the soil. Along with and even before the transformation of natural rent into money rent, arises a class of landless farm hands who work for hire. These laborers are mainly recruited from that class of serfs who were employed by well-to-do serfs during the feudal regime, while the well-to-do-serfs develop into capitalist farmers. A typical form of this transition to capitalism and of the difficulties standing in its way is presented by France before the great Revolution and has its theoretical spokesman in Quesnay and the physiocrats.

The capitalist theory of ground rent, however, is a specifically English product, and its historical cradle is very naturally found in England for the reason that it was there that ground rent first passed over into a mode of production, which began to differentiate rent of land from industrial profit and banker's interest.

The capitalist mode of production is conditioned on the separation of the agricultural producer from his bonds to the feudal lord, and in general on the expropriation of the mass of the laboring people from the soil.

"To this extent the monopoly of landed property is a historical premise, and remains the basis of the capitalist mode of production, just as it does of all other modes of production which rest on the exploitation of the masses in one form or another. But that form of landed property which the capitalist mode of production meets in its first stages, does not suit its requirements. It creates for itself that form of property in land which is adapted to its requirements, by subordinating agriculture to the dominion of capital. It transforms feudal landed property, tribal property, small peasants' property or *mark* communes, whatever may be their legal form, into the economic form corresponding to the requirements of capitalism." (Karl Marx, Capital, Volume III)

Already Adam Smith demonstrated that the ground rent paid in the production of minor crops and cattle is determined by the ground rent paid in the production of such staples as wheat and corn. And he clearly distinguished between capitalist's profits, landlord's rent, and laborer's wages. He was one of the first to warn economists against confounding these things and obliterating their economic significance by applying such terms as profit, rent, wages, indiscriminately to all surplus-value. But he was himself still struggling with the subject and suffering from the inconsistencies of his own position.

In the form given to it by Ricardo, the classic theory of ground rent is still full of inconsistencies and errors. The gist of his theory is that economic rent "is always the difference between the produce obtained by the employment of two equal quantities of capital and labor", and that "whatever diminishes the inequality of the produce obtained on the same or on new land, tends to lower rent and whatever increases that inequality, necessarily produces an opposite effect, and tends to raise it". (Ricardo, Principles of Political Economy) In brief, his idea of rent is merely that capitals invested in lands of different productivity and working with the same amount of money and labor produce different amounts of surplus-value and that whatever exceeds the surplus-value produced on the least productive land constitutes the rent, which the capitalist must hand over to the landlord.

In this form, the theory of ground rent does not explain the principal difficulties of capitalist production in agriculture, any more than Ricardo's theory of value was able to explain the difficulties of industrial surplus-value. It did not clearly define what kind of labor produced value and measured it, nor by what methods surplus-value is produced. Much less did it explain the formation of an average rate of profit, and the relation of this average rate of profit to the surplus-profit paid in the form of ground rent. Ricardo's theory of ground rent fails particularly in its appreciation of the fact that ground rent does not necessarily imply a gradual cultivation of worse and worse land (an idea which Henry George copied without further ado), but on the contrary that ground rent is very well compatible with a continual increase in the productivity of agriculture or a cultivation of better and better and better land.

Marx performed pioneer work on this ground just as he did in the field of industrial surplus-value. The Marxian theory of differential rent and absolute rent is the only really exhaustive and satisfactory theory which exists in political economy. Only after the question of the value and surplus-value of industrial capital and of the method of its realization in the circulation had been solved, was it possible to arrive at a solution of the question whence the landlord received the money for his rent and what determined the rate of ground rent.

The basis of Marx's theory of ground rent is his theory of the average rate of profit. The rate of agricultural profits under capitalism, according to him, is determined by the rate of industrial profit. Economic rent, in his sense of the term, means the surplus-profit made by the more productive agricultural capitals over and above the average profit realized by the least productive agricultural capital. The average price at which the products of this least productive agricultural capital are sold is equal to their price of production, that is, equal to their cost-price plus the average rate of profit. This price of production of the least productive agricultural capital is the regulating market-price for the products of all other kinds of land, whether they make more or less than the average profit. The law of value works among these capitals in the following general way:

Take four agricultural capitals of 50 shillings each with different rates of productivity. Let A, the least productive, produce one quarter of wheat at 60 shillings, making 10 shillings of profit, or 20 percent; let B produce two quarters of wheat, worth 120 shillings, making 70 shillings of profit, or 60 shillings of surplus-profit; let C produce 3 quarters of wheat, worth 180 shillings, 130 shillings of profit or 120 shillings of surplus-profit; let D produce four quarters of wheat, worth 240 shillings, a profit of 190 shillings, or a surplus-profit of 180 shillings. The total market-price of these four yields of wheat is then 60+ 120+ 180+ 240 = 600 shillings for 10 quarters of wheat. But the total price of production of these ten quarters of wheat is only four times 60, or 240 shillings, since each capital has a cost-price of only 50 shillings, to which the average profit of 10 shillings is added to make up their price of production. The market-value of these products is, therefore, larger than their total price of production. And this is the effect of capitalist competition, the social method of determining the market-values of all products.

This is but a general illustration of the way in which the rate of ground rent (or agricultural surplus-profit) is determined. Marx supplies in his work many other illustrations, dealing specifically with the different possibilities of this problem. We need not go into such details here. It is sufficient here to make the reader familiar with the general idea. Whether this general idea is applied to different rates of productivity obtained one after another on the same land or simultaneously on different lands, this theory will suffice for all practical purposes. We must not look for mathematical exactness in the working out of economic laws, any more than we can arrive at absolute exactness in the working out of algebraic formulae in higher mathematics.

The general rule following from Marx's theory of ground rent is that capitalist ground rent (surplus-profit) increases absolutely on all lands, although the increase is not proportional to the increase in the invested capital. Taking the entire capital invested productively in land (old and additional capital) as a basis of calculation, the rate of ground rent decreases; but the absolute mass of surplus-profit increases; in like manner the decreasing rate of industrial profit is generally combined with an absolute increase of the mass of industrial profit. And this law holds good, with corresponding modifications, whether the prices of production of these capitals are rising or falling.

The ground rent proceeding in the form of surplus-profits from productive capitals must not be confounded with other kinds of rent which exist side by side with it. Capitalist ground rent is due primarily to the productivity of labor and of the soil. In the last analysis, it must be attributed to the fertility of the soil, for without it there would be no basis for any surplus-profit over and above the average rate of industrial profit, which is the foundation of the entire law of ground rent.

The law of the average rate of industrial profit implies that industrial capitals get, as a rule, only the average profit, and that industrial surplus-profits are an exception. The law of ground rent, on the other hand, implies that agricultural surplus-profits are the rule, and that no capital is invested in agriculture unless it pays at least the average profit, so that additional capital invested must bring more than the average profit, otherwise no additional capital would be invested. This agricultural surplus-profit cannot be due, in the last analysis, to any other cause than the fertility of the soil or natural powers such as waterpower, for which the capitalist pays nothing, any more than any capitalist pays anything for the average profit which he realizes. And the increasing fertility of the soil is as much a premise for the increase of the mass of agricultural surplus-profit, as the increase in the productivity of labor is a premise for the growth of the mass of average profit.

This capitalist ground rent may be, and generally is, complicated with other forms of rent, which represent modified survivals of older forms. But these modified older forms are all subject to the movement of modern capitalist rent, and are in the last resort determined by it.

The price of land under capitalism is generally regarded by bourgeois economists as a capitalization of land value, and its rent represents so much interest on money invested in ownership. But the rate of prices is determined by the interest derived from the ownership of land which is productively exploited and yields a surplus-profit, a capitalist ground rent. Only when this capitalist ground rent is explained can other forms of rent, such as money rent in the form of interest, be explained. Rent on land used unproductively (as a site for a dwelling place or an office) is determined in the last analysis by the rent of productive land. To explain land values, or interest drawn from capitalized land values, by their own capitalization, as some would-be economists are trying to do, is like explaining industrial profit by the self-capitalization of money.

"The mistaking ground rent for the interest form, which it assumes for the buyer of land . . . must lead to the most absurd conclusions. Since landed property is considered, in all old countries, as a particularly noble form of property, and its purchase also as an eminently safe investment of capital, the rate of interest at which ground rent is bought is generally lower than that of other investments of capital for a long time, so that a buyer of real estate draws, for instance, only 4 percent on his purchase price, whereas he would draw 5 percent for the same capital in other investments. In other words, he pays more capital for the ground rent than he would for the same amount of income in other investments. This leads Mr. Thiers to conclude in his utterly valueless work on La Propriété . . . that ground rent is low, while it proves merely that its purchase price is high. . . To derive from the sale and purchase of ground rent a justification for its existence signifies to justify its existence by its existence." (Karl Marx, Capital, Volume III)

While the worst land does not yield any ground rent, it may yield profits on capital. Since ground rent signifies here only the difference between the average profit and the surplus-profit realized in capitalist agriculture, it is based on the assumption that the worst land must produce at least the average profit. A capitalist farmer exploiting laborers on such land must reproduce his constant capital plus his variable capital plus the average profit and sell his product at the average price of production. But he will not make any surplus-profit, and the land will not yield any ground rent.

But how can a capitalist farmer get access to such land without paying rent?

In the first place, he may be the owner of such land and exploit it with his own capital. Marx considers this as an exception under capitalism.

In the second place, the capitalist farmer may pay ground rent for land, only a part of which actually yields a surplus-profit. But so long as he can make the average profit on the remainder of the land, he will cultivate this also.

In the third place, a capitalist farmer may invest accumulated capital (additional capital) in land for which he pays ground rent, and this additional capital may yield only the average profit, while the reproduced original capital continues to yield a surplus-profit. He pays ground rent out of the proceeds of his original capital, but not of his additional capital.

But such exceptions from the rule are a confirmation of Marx's theory of ground rent, not a refutation of it. They cannot be explained, unless the rule is first explained.

Neither is the Marxian theory of ground rent refuted by the fact that the products of land whose productivity does not yield any economic rent, may be sold under exceptional market conditions above the average price of production, so that a surplus-profit is actually realized on them. For in the first place, this surplus-profit is not due to the productivity of the land, but to exceptional opportunities in circulation. In the second place, even such opportunities cannot be explained on any other basis but that of the Marxian theory of industrial profit and ground rent. Such exceptions are explained only by the rule that the average price of production is actually the standard around which all market prices fluctuate.

If the regulating market price of the products of the soil is not the average price of production (cost-price of capitalist plus average profit), but rather a price which is equal to the average price of production plus a certain amount for rent, then this rent is not economic rent in the strict meaning of this term, but "absolute" ground rent, derived from the ownership of the land itself. But even so, this absolute ground rent can be explained only by the law of differential rent, or ground rent proper. It signifies that the monopoly of land can enforce an increase of prices of production over and above the average which regulates differential rent.

In practice this amounts to saying that agricultural products may be sold above their price of production and below their value, just as the price of production of industrial commodities may be above or below their value and, as a rule, does not coincide with their value.

All the complications to which the capitalist mode of production gives rise by creating new forms of rent and transforming and dominating survivals of old forms, require for their theoretical solution the understanding of the "pure" form, through which capitalism expresses its typical tendencies and enforces its prevailing law — the law of value.

Marx alone has found the key to all these problems.

Once that we understand the Marxian law of value and the significance of the different roles played by constant and variable capital in production or by the circulation of value, we can readily grasp the fact that fixed capital invested in the soil, unlike fixed capital invested in industrial machinery, etc., increases in value in proportion as the soil is treated scientifically, so that this fixed capital becomes, through the peculiar productivity of the soil, an element in yielding surplus-value over and above the average and producing different forms of rent.

There have been at all times thinkers who have tried to conceal economic lines of cleavage by a sentimental reconciliation of antagonisms on paper. Economic theories are not free from such attempts. The Ricardian theory of ground rent, which laid bare the antagonism between industrial capitalists and landlords, was combated by economists like Carey, who tried to represent rent as interest on capital, similar to interest on loaned money. This was equivalent to making capitalists of landlords and wiping out the line of economic cleavage between landlords and capitalists. But the bitter reality of capitalist development laughed Carey to scorn and called forth fierce struggles between these two economic classes.

In modern times, Henry George has made a similar attempt by garbling the Ricardian theory of ground rent into an indefinite theory of land values, and making of this distorted classic theory a blanket by which to cover the class-struggle between proletarians and capitalists. I do not mean to insinuate that this was George's open intention. But his theory practically works in this direction. It is evident that this attempt, like Carey's, must come to grief in proportion as the class-struggle goes its inexorable way and lights the revolutionary fires which must consume the economic foundations of both landlordism and capitalism.

Chapter 18   Profit, Interest And Rent Under Capitalist Competition

Looking upon the process of industrial capitalism as one immense co-operative movement, we shall see that value and surplus-value are produced nowhere but in the sphere of production, including such other departments as act as intermediary links between production and circulation, for instance, the transportation industry. When the commodities, charged with their value and surplus-value, finally reach the circulation and have a certain money-price, an addition may, indeed, be made to their price in the shape of cost of handling, storing, etc., as we have seen in the preceding chapter. But this is an addition of value only from the point of view of the individual capitalists who invest money and pay wage laborers in the processes of handling, storing etc. From the point of view of society as a whole, the addition of the cost of such unproductive labor to the price of commodities is not a production of value, but an expenditure of unproductive labor and capital, even if it is an addition to the price of commodities, which is inevitable. At any rate it is evident that any addition to the price of commodities in the sphere of circulation which is not due to productive labor cannot add any value from the standpoint of the entire capitalist process, but merely increases the cost of commodities to the consumer and must be paid out of already existing value, such as the profits of the capitalist consumer or the wages of the working class consumer.

Whether commodities are sold in the sphere of circulation at the values which they originally brought with them from the sphere of production, or at some other price, depends in no way on the caprice of the individual capitalist or merchant. On the market, competition sways the scale. And competition itself is subject to the law of value, as the capitalist would easily see if he were interested in economic problems sufficiently to bother his head about them.

The capitalist calculates his profits on the total (constant and variable) capital invested by him in the production of a certain quantity of commodities. He figures both constant and variable capital as one lump sum of money, which he calls his cost-price. He does not consider the surplus-value at all which the commodities contain, but adds to his cost-price a certain amount, which varies according to the latitude permitted to him by competition, and this addition to his cost-price he calls his profit. Where this profit comes from, he does not care. In his opinion, society as a whole has at certain periods a definite amount of money at its disposal, and the more he can add to the cost-price of his commodities, the more of the available money-supply can he gather into his strongbox.

But the scientific explorer cannot calculate in this manner. He cannot stick to the surface of things. He must probe the problems of economics to the very bottom. So long as the law of value is accepted as the regulating force of capitalist production, we must find another explanation than that of the capitalist for his profits and for the fact that he cannot make his profits arbitrarily as high as he wants to.

According to the Marxian theories of value and surplus-value, the price of commodities, as expressed in money, cannot be composed of anything but the value of the constant plus the value of the variable capital plus as much of the surplus-value as competition will permit the capitalist to realize in the shape of profit. If the commodities are sold at the full value which they bring with them from the sphere of production then the capitalist's profit will be equal to the surplus-value contained in his commodities. If the commodities are sold above or below their full value, then the capitalist will realize more or less than the surplus-value contained in them.

It is evident that the composition of the value of a commodity must, under these circumstances, be dependent upon the composition of the capital with which it has been produced. If surplus-value is produced only by the labor of the productive workers, not by the dead labor incorporated in the instruments and materials bought with the constant capital, then the proportion of the variable to the constant capital must play a very important role in the final struggle of the capitalist for the surplus-value taken to the sphere of circulation. The value of the commodities of the capitalist must fluctuate in proportion to the quantity of surplus-value which he can create by means of the variable capital invested in labor-power, and the quantity of machinery and raw materials which this labor-power can consume productively in the labor process.

The composition of capital includes both the value and the material substance of constant and variable capital. The value refers to the proportion between variable and constant elements of value, the material substance refers to the materials incorporated in means of production, raw materials, and living labor-power. Marx calls the former the "value-composition", the latter the "technical composition" of capital. Both of these compositions are intimately related and influence one another. Marx calls their joint result the "organic composition" of capital.

When the capitalist mode of production develops out of feudalism, it opens the way to capitals of widely varying organic composition. Different capitalists, therefore, turn out products whose value-composition differs from that of their competitors, because all of them work with varying quantities of material elements of value, and therefore, of surplus-value.

The capitalists figure their so-called cost-price in money, not in the labor-cost which is the real basis of all social exchange-values. But we know that the value of the metals in money is itself determined by the quantity of socially necessary average labor required to produce them. What we call the cost-price of commodities is, therefore, something different from the cost-price of the capitalist. We figure the cost-price of products by the dead and living labor incorporated in them, while the capitalist figures merely the money which he spent in the production of his commodities.

Our method of determining the value of commodities by their labor-cost enables us to find out just how much dead and living labor is incorporated in them and just how this proportion of dead and living labor in them agrees with the average labor socially necessary to produce a certain commodity.

The average labor-cost necessary to produce a certain commodity is always the prevailing cost, which determines the price of this commodity on the market. It represents the average value of the constant and variable elements of capital required under the prevailing conditions of production, and the surplus-value turned out with them. It is found by taking the average of all individual compositions of capital in the sphere producing this commodity.

Let us assume that the average composition of capitals producing cotton yarn is 80 constant plus 20 variable capital, and that the rate of surplus-value (calculated on the variable capital) is 100 per cent. Then each 100 of these capitals will turn out a product whose value will be composed of 80 C+ 20 V + 20 S = 120. In other words, $20 of each 100 pay for labor-power, and $80 for wear and tear of machinery and raw materials. If one hour of average social labor is worth 50ct, then $20 will pay for 40 hours of average social labor. But the laborers work 80 hours instead of 40, and the value of the 40 hours of surplus-labor is likewise $20. The capitalist does not pay for this surplus-labor, but pockets its value in his profit. How much cotton yarn do these 80 hours of labor turn out? Let us assume for the sake of easy figuring that the $80 for constant capital are composed of $10 for wear and tear of spindles, and $70 for cotton. Let one spindle be worth $10, then one spindle is worn out in 80 hours of labor. Let cotton be worth 10c a pound, then $70 will buy 700 pounds of cotton. These 700 pounds of cotton make 700 pounds of yarn (we leave the question of waste out of consideration), so that 80 working hours turn out 700 pounds of yarn, at a value of $120.

This is the average price at which cotton yarn is sold (at wholesale) under the prevailing conditions of yarn manufacture, and the capitalists working with capitals of this average composition make a profit of 20ct on the dollar.

Now let us assume that a few capitalists have invested capitals which have a different composition than most other capitals in this industry. Let a few have a higher organic composition, and a few a lower one.

Take it that the organic composition of the more highly organized capitals is 90 constant plus 10 variable capital, but that the rate of surplus-value is the same as that of all other capitals in the same industry, that is 100 percent, so that the laborers throughout the cotton yarn industry work one half of the time to produce their wages and the other half to produce surplus-value for the capitalists. Then the value of the product of these capitals will be 90 C + 10 V + 10 S = 110. Since one hour of this labor is worth 50ct, $10 pay for 20 hours of it, and the laborers work 40 hours to work up $90 worth of machinery and raw materials. Let the proportion between wear and tear and cotton be $10 worth of spindle and $80 worth of cotton. This means that these laborers, by the help of better machinery, work up 800 pounds of cotton in 40 hours, whereas the laborers of the capitalists with capitals of average composition work up only 700 pounds of cotton in 80 hours. If the laborers of these capitalists with more productive capitals worked 80 hours, the same as the laborers of the other capitalists, they would turn out 1,600 pounds of cotton, and the value of this cotton would be $220, of which $20 would be surplus-value. The total cost to the capitalists would be $200 during these 80 working hours, but their product would be 200 pounds of yarn more than that of the capitalists consuming $100 worth in 80 hours. But this is not the only advantage which the favored capitalists get. Cotton yarn sells at 120 per 700 pounds. In that case the better-situated capitalists have an advantage whether demand and supply balance one another or not. If the demand for cotton is equal to the supply, so that all the yarn is taken which can be produced, then the favored capitalists can sell their yarn at $120 for 700 pounds, or $274.29 for 1,600 pounds, and pocket $74.29 of profits in the same time that their competitors with average capitals pocket $20. If the demand exceeds the supply, the situation will be the same. And if the supply of cotton yarn exceeds the demand for it, the capitalists with capitals of higher organic composition will be able to undersell their competitors to a point where the less favored capitalists must either sell at a total loss, or stop producing cotton yarn. For instance, the favored capitalists could offer 1,600 pounds of cotton at a total price of $220, or 800 pounds of yarn at a total price of $110, and still make a profit of $10 per each $100 invested, while the capitalists who can offer only 700 pounds of yarn at a price of $120, if compelled to sell at the price of the favored capitalists, would not only lose their entire profit, but even a part of their invested capital.

Take it, finally, that a few capitals in the manufacture of cotton yarn are still working with a capital of a lower than average composition, say with 60 C + 40 V, but that their laborers also work half of the day to produce their wages, and half of the day to produce surplus-value. Then the value of their product (including surplus-value) would be 60 C + 40 V + 40 S = 140. In other words, they must pay $40 or the equivalent of 80 hours of labor for wages, their employees must work 160 hours to consume productively $60 worth of machinery and raw materials, and if the proportion between wear and tear and cotton were $10 for wear and tear of spindles and $50 for cotton, these laborers would work up only 500 pounds of cotton in 180 hours, making 500 pounds of yarn, and this yarn would have to be sold at the rate of $17.14 per hundred pounds even under the most favorable conditions, in which the demand would absorb all the yarn produced. They would have to sell their 500 pounds of yarn for $85.70, whereas it has a value of $140 and cost them $100 to produce that value. They would lose not only their entire profit of $40, but also $14.30 of their capital, and their employees would have worked twice as long as the laborers of the capitalists with capitals of average composition, and four times as long as those of the capitalists with capitals of higher than average composition. Under these circumstances the capitalists with capitals of lower than average composition would have to suspend operations.

The same rule which holds good for the capitals of a certain industry prevails in society at large and subjects all capitals to the sway of the law of value. The capitals of average composition everywhere determine the average price at which commodities are to be sold, the capitals with higher than average composition can either make a greater profit than the average or sell at the value of their own products and undersell all competitors with more lowly organized capitals, while the capitals with a lower than the average composition are ruled out of competition entirely. If the composition of the exceptional capitals with a higher organic constitution becomes general, then this is the average composition, the prices of commodities fall, and new improvements in machinery and productivity of labor are required to secure more than the average profit. It does not matter how much surplus-value the individual capitalist may produce. He does not share in the profits of the entire capitalist process in proportion to the surplus-value produced by his own working men, but in proportion to the total capital invested by him, and his capital is merely a definite percentage in the total capital of society. Commodities are regulated on the market by the average price of production, that is, the cost-price (the value of constant plus variable capital) plus the average profit, and only capitals with a higher than an average composition can secure a surplus-profit above the average, so long as they occupy this exceptional position (irregularities always excepted). In other words, commodities are, as a rule, not sold at their values.

Only so long as the prevailing conditions of production permit the capitals of average composition to sell all their products, that is, so long as supply and demand balance one another or demand exceeds supply, do these capitals sell their products at their value, while all others sell either above or below their value. And generally speaking, commodities are sold at their value only so long as we look upon society as a whole, and all capitals as one capital, because in that case the advantage of some is a loss to others, and the final result is merely a different distribution of values and surplus-values among different capitalists. But from the point of view of individual capitalists, or individual industries, commodities are almost never sold at their value. The law of value merely enforces itself through an endless series of fluctuations, whose average is never stable and can never be reduced to any mathematical exactness. The competition of capitals of different organic composition, and the necessity of yielding a part of the industrial profits to merchants and bankers, continually strive to break through the law of value, and it maintains itself only through an indeterminable struggle of averages.

Whether a capital is productively invested in industrial pursuits, or unproductively in stores, banks, or whether it is invested in agriculture or in real estate and buildings, it can, as a rule, secure only the average profit prevailing in society as a whole, and interest and rent must follow the fluctuations of this average profit. Where they do not follow these fluctuations, exceptional rates of interest and rent must be explained by the law of value, the same as the average profit itself.

In short, so long as capitalist production lasts, the law of value cannot express itself normally but must enforce itself through fluctuations around a variable average. Only under a socialist system of production can the Marxian theory of value be consistently applied and used as a regulator of collective production.

Chapter 19   The Drift Of Industrial Capitalism

So long as merchants' capital is the prevailing form of capital, and so long as the accumulation of money serves mainly as a lever for lifting more and more surplus-products out of the sphere of production without touching the mechanism of this sphere itself, the precapitalist foundations of human societies remain very stable.

But the practices of the feudal aristocracy in cooperation with the manipulations of the merchants and financiers transform feudal peasants into proletarians with no other marketable property but their labor-power, separate the handicraftsmen from the feudal employees, widen the field of production for the better situated middle classes, and strengthen the hands of the city merchants more and more against the aggressions of the feudal aristocracy.

When the craftmaster, the well-to-do serf, the banker, the merchant, the lord, the churchman become manufacturers, when the landless serf and journeyman become wage slaves, when capital in the form of money invades the sphere of production and wrenches it loose from its old foundations, then a new law of development seizes all forms of accumulated money, turns the tide of history into new channels, and hastens the speed of its flow.

Merchants' capital required thousands of years to extend its operations in the sphere of circulation from the narrow strip of the primitive *mark* to the interurban mart and the international emporium. Industrial capital engulfs both the spheres of production and circulation in less than three centuries. The nineteenth century alone, under the lash of industrial capitalism, has carried the human race over more ground than all the preceding millenniums in which other forms of capital developed.

The ancient and medieval forms of capital existed chiefly by virtue of the surplus thrown off by the sphere of production after the wants of the producers had been satisfied. Industrial capital starts out by making the producers subservient to its need of self-expansion and placing the satisfaction of this need above the satisfaction of the wants of the produces. Man becomes the tool of capital.

The market, once a place of minor importance for the productive basis of social life, now becomes the center of all productive activity. The whole world of organic and inorganic, movable and immovable things, love, virtue, honor, and eternal salvation, are turned into commodities and thrown upon the market in order to "make money". The profits of the capitalist, formerly a mere side issue from the point of view of social progress, become the all-absorbing incentive and regulator of history. The accumulation of industrial money-capital, and the immanent law of its development, assume the role of social pilots and steer the ship of mankind over the reckless course of profits, coining more profits out of human flesh and blood.

In the beginning of capitalism it is mainly the working class that feels the inexorable hand of capitalist development. And it is this class which receives the hardest blows from the results of the capitalist law of accumulation, so long as capitalism lasts. But the ruling classes are by no means exempt from its uncontrolled fury. In proportion as capitalism develops, it is brought home with increasing persistence and directness even to the capitalist mind that capital is stronger than the capitalist, and that capital in its turn is subject to laws of its own mechanical making which it cannot control.

The farther capitalism proceeds upon its historical road, the more heavily do its uncontrolled laws fall upon the capitalist himself. They become dangerous to his existence, compel him to resist this danger by opposing the natural direction of the development from which they spring, and thereby to undermine capital itself and to hasten his own downfall. The same laws which built up the structure of capitalism during its ascending period, turn during its descending curve into means of destroying it and the capitalist class.

To the same extent do these laws turn from destructive enemies of the working class into constructive aids to its organization, education and supremacy, although they never cease to press hard upon the workers. Every capitalist wants to make as much profit as possible. In order to make profit, he must squeeze surplus-value out of his employees and sell the products containing it in the competitive market. The more surplus-value he can filch from his employees, the greater will be his opportunity to gather profits from the sale of his commodities. Surplus-value cannot be increased by any other means than that of increasing the intensity of labor together with its productivity, or of increasing the surplus-labor at the expense of the necessary labor, or of prolonging the working day, or by using all these means together.

Not all means of intensifying exploitation have the same value in the mechanical working of the turn-over of capital. The prolongation of the working day beyond its normal length, and thus the production of absolute surplus-value, are more typical of the beginnings of capitalist production, although they never disappear entirely even in the most advanced stages of capitalism. Later, when the proletariat has become sufficiently organized to resist the exactions of the capitalists, this method of surplus-production is more and more narrowed down and used by the small capitalist rather than large industrial corporations. It is more and more restricted and eclipsed by the production of relative surplus-value through the intensification of the productive labor during the normal working day and the displacement of hand labor by machine labor.

The most effective means of intensifying the productive power of labor within the limits of the normal working day is the introduction of improved machinery and the progressive increase of the speed of its revolutions. This is the most significant and characteristic method by which capitalism succeeds in increasing the surplus-labor compared to the necessary labor during the normal working day of a certain period.

It is only the variable capital which is the really active capital under capitalism. But in order to increase the effectiveness of his variable capital, the industrial capitalist must invest more and more money in productive machinery. In proportion as the accumulation of surplus-value proceeds, a relatively larger and larger portion of it is, therefore, invested in machinery, while a relatively smaller and smaller portion is added to the variable capital.

The variable and the constant capital both increase continually and with them increases the mass of surplus-value (calculated on the variable capital) and the mass of profits (calculated on the total constant plus variable capital). As a rule, the rate of surplus-value (rate of exploitation) increases at the same time. But the constant capital increases faster than the variable capital, and the difference between the mass of produced commodities and their value increases faster than that between the constant and variable capital. The inevitable result of this is that the rate of profit must have a tendency to fall, even though the rate of surplus-value is rising and the mass of profits increasing.

Take for instance three different capitals of different organic composition, such as we compared in the previous chapter. Let us assume that instead of competing with one another all at the same period, they represent the average composition of the social capital at three different periods of capitalist development.

Let the capital of 60 C + 40 V represent the rule in the beginning years of capitalism; let the capital of 80 C+ 20 V be the average during the middle period of capitalism; and let the capital of 90 C + 10 V show the average composition of the social capital in the declining years of capitalism. Let us assume, for the sake of easy comparison, that all these capitals work with the same rate of exploitation, and that all of them turn over their entire constant and variable capital inside of one year. In reality this is hardly ever the case, but it will do for the present comparison. Then we get the following values for the product of these capitals, assuming the rate of surplus-value to be 100 percent:

60 C + 40 V + 40 S = 140

80 C + 20 V + 20 S = 120

90 C + 10 V + 10 S = 110

In all of these cases, the rate of surplus-value is 100 percent. But the rate of profit declines in proportion as the constant capital increases over the variable capital. During the first period, the rate of profit is 40 percent; during the second period it is 20 percent; during the last period it is 10 percent. We have already seen, however, that this declining rate of profit may, and does, go hand in hand with a rise in the mass of profit, so that the capitalists pocket more profit even though the rate of profit declines.

Simple as these three formulas may appear, they are the handwriting on the wall which presages the downfall of capitalism. Let us look at them a little closer. They reveal a good deal more than the first glance of them shows.

In the first place, they show that the constant capital has a tendency to increase faster than the variable capital; in the second place they show that the rate of profit declines; in the third place they indicate that the chances of employment do not increase as fast for the working class as the constant capital of the capitalist increases; in the fourth place they reveal that capital is concentrated, in other words, that the scale of production is continually expanded; in the fifth place they show that small capitals cannot stand the competition of large ones, because it requires plenty of money to increase the constant capital by buying improved machinery and large quantities of raw materials; and finally they show that concentration of capital goes hand in hand with a centralization of capital, that is, with an elimination of small capitalists and the accumulation of larger and larger capitals in the hands of the surviving great capitalists.

Concentration and centralization of capital sound the doom of the middle class as a socially essential element in production, although this class never disappears entirely, but merely changes its character by being transformed from independent producers into dependent agents and employees of the great capitalists. In proportion as the middle class loses its importance in the process of social production, the great capitalists and the working proletariat become the typical representatives of capitalism.

The relative decrease in the chances of employment for the working class assumes on the surface the aspect of an increase of the working class population over the means of subsistence. A vaster and vaster unemployed problem thus threatens the security of the capitalist foundations.

This is a direct result of the mechanism of capitalist production. But the mechanism of the sphere of circulation adds its share to complicate the situation for the ruling class.

The competition of capitalists among themselves and the elimination of the weaker capitalists leads not only to a centralization of instruments of production, but also to a centralization of money in the hands of fewer and fewer magnates. To the extent that this centralization of means of production and money continues, the unemployed problem is intensified. It is true that the increase of the mass of profits (despite the decrease of the rate of profits) compels the successful capitalists temporarily to enter new avenues of investment and thus to open more opportunities for employment to the reserve army of unemployed. But this merely defers the final reckoning, because the new fields of investment necessarily develop the same tendencies as the old ones, as monopolies in the hands of giant corporations gobble up the dispersed and formerly neglected lines of minor importance. The end cannot be anything else but still vaster unemployed problems.

The permanent existence of an army of unemployed increases the competition of laborers for jobs, and this naturally tends to keep wages at the lowest level of subsistence and to check the fall of the rate of profit, so that the question of the investment of the mass of new profits becomes ever more pressing for the capitalists. On the other hand, the keeping of wages at the lowest level of subsistence threatens periodically to wreck the entire capitalist system, because the working people are the principal consumers, and they cannot begin to absorb the immense quantity of goods made by them as the productivity of labor increases, for the simple reason that their wages, even if permanently above the average (a thing which is as rare as an honest capitalist politician) are an equivalent for but a small part of the total value of the social product.

So long as capitalism is young, production is wholly planless and wild. And since the fixed portions of the constant capital differ in their turn-over from the circulating portions, production begins to lag, its wheels soon become clogged here and there, the markets are quickly glutted, and every few years a commercial crisis stops the wheels of production. The capitalists cannot reproduce their capital, their machinery and raw materials deteriorate for want of the conserving and life-giving power of labor, their profits stop, and confusion reigns in the capitalist camp. Meanwhile the working people, thrown out of employment, stand hungry, shivering and ragged before mountains of wealth produced by them, waiting for the magic word which shall recall them to their servitude and fill their stomachs.

A period of stagnation follows the acute stage of a commercial crisis, the unemployed become troublesome, crime, suicide, disease and insanity are rampant, and the entire forces of capitalist suppression are feverishly busy at all points to punish the miserable for the sins of the capitalists and shield the capitalists from the evils of their own making.

More and more labor saving machinery is produced in the frenzied rush after more profits and a rapid turn-over of capital. Little do the capitalists realize that the mere acceleration of the turn-over of capital does not increase their profits, unless other causes have first increased the intensity of exploitation and the creation of surplus-value. They look astonished when confronted with the fact that a capital of $100, if turned over more quickly by underselling competitors, does not bring any more profits by such rapid turn-overs than the capital of a competitor turned over once in the same time and selling commodities at the average market price.

Yet that is actually a fact. Take two capitals of $100 each. Let the average rate of profit be 20 percent. Let the capital of A be turned over once in twelve months, and the capital of B ten times in twelve months. But how is this tenfold turn-over of B's capital possible? B must undersell his competitor A. Each has $120 worth of commodities. A sells his commodities at their average price of production, that is, at $120, and at the end of twelve months he has turned over his capital and pocketed $20 of profit. B sells his commodities below their price of production, in order to turn his capital over faster. He sells at $102, and turns over his capital once while A has sold only one tenth of his commodities. B reproduces his capital, manufactures another batch of commodities and sells again at $ 102. Now he has pocketed $4.00 of profit. And so on eight times more. At the end of ten turn-overs he has pocketed exactly $20 of profit, not a cent more than A with one turn-over per year realizes. Evidently a rapid turn-over of capital by itself does not make profits any higher.

In reality the capitalist does not rely merely on a rapid turn-over of his capital. He rather tries to beat down the rate of wages, so that he can increase the creation of surplus-value. Along with the introduction of labor-saving machinery comes, therefore, the employment of women and children instead of able-bodied men, and the lowering of the scale of wages to a point where even a child can barely keep flesh and bones together.

As the world market widens, as production is better regulated by centralized control, the cycle of commercial crisis becomes longer and longer and is gradually lengthened into periods of protracted depression. When the home market becomes permanently unable, in spite of the increase of the population, to assimilate the overproduction of commodities (overproduction, not because there is more than can be consumed, but because there is an underconsumption of goods on the part of the working class), the theater of capitalist competition spreads over the entire globe. Wild wars are undertaken for the conquest of new markets and new fields of production.

Centralization of control over large industries may lessen the acuteness and frequency of commercial crises and financial panics, so far as they are due to the mechanical and spontaneous action of disorderly production and circulation. But it opens the way for the conscious promotion of commercial crises and financial panics, because the control of vast fields of production and of the money supply enables the great corporations to close down their factories at will and lock out immense armies of working people, to manipulate the money-market, and involve the entire nation in their squabbles over the control of special fields of exploitation. These conscious attempts at commercial crises and panics are no longer of such nature as to shake the entire foundation of capitalism and ruin large numbers of socially essential capitalists. They are rather maneuvers made with the intention of squeezing the little capitalists and stockholders, who are more hangers-on of the great capitalists than a socially independent and essential class.

At the same time, the growth of vast labor organizations threatens to rend the whole society into two warring camps. The class struggle between the proletariat and the great capitalists gradually overshadows all the artificial issues which the ruling classes have invented to divide the laboring classes among themselves.

Monopolies in the hands of great corporations (trusts) may check the tendency of rate of profit to fall (1) by depressing wages below the average-value of labor-power; (2) by selling commodities above their value; (3) by systematizing all modes of adulteration and eliminating waste; (4) by pressing upon the money-market, eliminating competition and preventing the lowering of profits and interest through it; (5) by suppressing new inventions which would tend to cheapen commodities, while the existing machinery is still able to supply more than the demands of the national and international markets; (6) by fomenting wars and thereby putting new life into "prosperity".

Yet at the same time monopolist corporations must bow to the dictates of international competition. They may temporarily dodge some of the worst "evils" which strike hard at capitalism; they may circumvent in a greater or lesser degree the law of value; they may secure a short respite for themselves and their class from the social laws that have pronounced sentence upon them. But the end must be inevitably the same. The question, what to do with the increasing mass of profits, how to harmonize the working of collective production and distribution with the individual or class ownership of the essential sources of life, how to meet the demands of the increasing number of homeless, jobless, starving laborers, must finally be answered. The capitalist class has no satisfactory answer. Only the working class can solve this problem.

The same general tendencies which undermine the foundation of capitalism in industrial life, also appear in the development of agriculture under capitalism. Concentration and centralization of agricultural capital do not proceed in exactly the same way as they do in industrial production, but the result is the same. Land may not be monopolized to such an extent as the industrial means of production. Agricultural capitalism has not, so far, eliminated the small farm or rendered it economically of minor significance, as industrial capitalism has done with the industrial middle class. The number of small farms, at least in the United States has rather increased, and with them the number of middle class farmers. So long as it pays the capitalists who control the productive life of the nation, to leave the small farmer in virtual possession, if not in actual control, of his land and home, and to exploit him in the sphere of circulation rather than in the sphere of production, it will be done. Still the tendency is here also to transfer more and more of the productive functions from the farm to the industrial field, and to leave only such purely agricultural work in the hands of the tillers of the soil as cannot be divorced from the land. The manufacture of butter, the distribution of milk, the skimming of cream, disappear from the farm. Improved machinery, which the farmer must have if he would keep step with the demands of capitalist production, enable the manufacturer of farm implements and machinery to take large slices out of the farmer's income. The great transportation companies open their rapacious maws for him. Moneylenders secure a strangle hold on him. As a rule nothing remains for him but the exhausting toil in the fields and the illusion, that he is still his own boss and the master of his own fate. So far as interest depends upon the industrial profit, and the rate of interest upon the rate of industrial profit, it is evident that the rate of interest will have a tendency to fall with the average rate of industrial profit. But since the productivity of labor in the mining of precious metals and the centralization of money into fewer and fewer hands, together with the concentration of industries, accumulates vast funds of loanable capital seeking investment at profitable rates, the plethora of money has by itself a tendency to lower the rate of interest, so long as competition is still in force, even without the influence of the average rate of profit.

Where ground rent assumes the form of interest on money, the same tendency will appear and it will require a larger and larger capital to secure possession of real estate with a view to drawing a revenue or profit from it. The value of land will rise. So far as ground rent is a surplus-profit above the average on capitals invested in agriculture, we have already seen that the average rate of profit controls its movements, so that here, likewise, more and more capital is required to secure the same ground rent and the value of land will rise.

As the total population increases, the proportion between the different essential and unessential classes of society is gradually shifted. Speaking of classes as types of economic agents, the tendency is to increase the absolute number of members of all classes. But their relative proportions are altered in such a way that the number of great capitalists increases very slowly compared to all other classes, while the typical middle class of early capitalist society, composed of independent artisans, shop-keepers, little businessmen and small capitalists, gradually gives way to a different middle class, which is largely dependent upon the great corporations. Only the agricultural middle class preserves much of its old historical character, although it, too, comes more and more under the sway of the great capitalists, like all other classes. The industrial proletariat increases faster than all other classes.

Generally speaking, capitalist development increases the number of middle class capitalists, dependent trades people, capitalist farmers, faster than that of the great capitalists, but decreases the influence of this new middle class in social production; the number of farming tenants increases faster than that of "free" farmers, and the number of mortgaged farms increases faster than the number of unencumbered farms, and the industrial proletariat outstrips all other classes in growth of numbers and economic influence.

Bourgeois economists have struggled in vain to solve these problems. For centuries these questions have remained unanswered by them. Most of the bourgeois economists are still unable to answer them. Some have read their solution in Marx, bust very few are willing to admit this, or to agree that Marx has solved these problems. The greater number of university professors still answer the vexing problems of capitalist economics by the specious and embarrassed vagaries of their predecessors. Particularly is this the case when the discussion broaches such questions as the relation of wages to profits, or of profits to the working population in general, or such problems as that of the influence of the productivity of labor in the production of precious metals on the prices of other commodities, particularly on the price of labor-power.

When industrial capitalism had reached the stage where a vast proletariat supplied a superabundant number of wage workers to the capitalists and left an increasing army of hundreds of thousands unemployed during a part or the entire length of the year, the bourgeois economists searched for an explanation of this problem.

Here are some of the explanations which were passed on as the acme of economist science for centuries. Some professors took their scientific ideas from the preachers and claimed that God had ordained that so many proletarians should remain unemployed and starve to death or end as paupers in the treadmills or the jails. Another professor, a little shrewder and less clumsy than his pious colleague, declared that the amount of money available in a certain society for wages was unalterably fixed, so that only a definite portion of the working people could be employed at a time. Then, at a later period, when the idea of social growth had forced itself upon the minds of the bourgeois thinkers, and when it was apparent to the dullest of them that the amount of money available in a certain society for its various purposes was continually increasing or fluctuating between increase and decrease in response to the requirements of national and international trade, Malthus invented his theory of overpopulation, or rather, plagiarized some of his smarter colleagues and dressed their ideas up as his own invention. He claimed that the working people, improvident and shiftless as they are, were continually propagating themselves faster than the employed portion of society could produce means of subsistence. For this reason, Malthus says, there is always an overpopulation of working people, so that more of them need work than the good capitalists can employ, and more of them want food, clothing and shelter than the co-operative efforts of the employed can produce. The result, according to Malthus, is a chronic unemployed problem, starvation, misery, and all the evils attending such a condition. And this explanation was acclaimed as a great scientific discovery, at time when the granaries and stores were bursting with supplies while thousands were crying for food and homes.

No matter what kind of an explanation the bourgeois professors advanced, all of them agreed that it was the fault of the working people themselves if they were in a condition of want and misery, and some of them went so far as to proclaim openly that war, pestilence, famine, and the wholesale butchering of rebellious and desperate wretches were a scientific solution of the unemployed problem, because these scourges of mankind "thinned out the surplus-population". It was always the working people who were superfluous, never the capitalists and aristocrats.

The Marxian theory of value and capitalist accumulation explains the connection between variable capital, constant capital, profits, and an increasing population of unemployed so clearly and convincingly, that all but capitalist professors will agree to it. We have already indicated this connection and need not repeat it here

The relation of the precious metals to their role as money and to the value and price of all other commodities has caused the bourgeois professors no less headache. Even the analytical brain of a Ricardo broke down hopelessly before the problem of the relation of currency to the prices of commodities. Marx has treated this point fully in his

"Critique of Political Economy" and in Volume III of his "Capital". It interests us here only in its relation to the unemployed problem.

The value of gold and silver, like that of all other commodities, is determined by the average labor socially necessary to produce them under prevailing conditions. The value of gold and silver available in a certain country is, therefore, at any period, a definite amount determined by the social productivity of the laborers in these industries under the existing technical conditions. This value is changed only when the average time socially necessary for the production of gold and silver is changed. Their price is changed when the production of gold does not keep step with the wear and tear of the gold in circulation, or when it exceeds this wear and tear by exportation and importation, or other causes that may create an appreciable disproportion between supply and demand.

Not all gold enters into the circulation of commodities as coined money. By far the greater portion of the money used for the circulation of commodities is paper, checks, drafts, or credit. The total amount of gold and silver in a certain country cannot, therefore, have any direct influence upon the prices of other commodities, and it cannot have any influence at all upon the value of other commodities, because that value does not depend on the value of gold, but on the necessary and surplus-labor incorporated in the commodities themselves. Gold and silver serve as measures of value only because social labor is embodied in them, and this labor in gold and silver is compared with the labor in the other commodities. The relation which bourgeois economists claimed to have discovered between the fall or rise in the value of gold, and the fall and rise in the value of other commodities, or the influence which they believed was exerted by the greater or smaller quantity of gold and silver in a certain country upon the prices of all other commodities, do not exist in fact.

Marx has supplied us with a convincing refutation of this old currency principle, which misled even the smartest bourgeois economists. He calls this principle "the old fib, which asserts that changes in the quantity of gold existing in a certain country, by increasing or reducing the quantity of the medium of circulation in that country, must raise or lower the prices of commodities in it". According to this currency principle, the prices of commodities were supposed to rise in that country into which gold is imported, and this is supposed to enhance the value of the commodities exported from the gold exporting to the gold importing country. On the other hand, the value of the commodities exported from the gold importing to the gold exporting country is supposed to fall in that case. But Marx has clearly demonstrated that the reduction of the quantity of gold in a certain country raises only the rate of interest, while an increase in the quantity of gold lowers this rate. And if the fluctuations of the rate of interest were not taken into account in the determination of the cost-price of commodities, or in the regulation of prices by demand and supply, there would not even be an indirect influence of the gold exports and imports upon the prices of commodities in any country.

It follows, therefore, that no matter how much or how little gold exists in a certain country, the unemployed are not concerned in it at all. The capitalist system of production requires a certain amount of circulating medium, or money, for the circulation of its commodities, and since there is never enough gold or silver in any country to supply the circulation, the missing amount is supplied by paper money, bank checks and credit.

"So long as enlightened bourgeois economy treats of 'capital' in its official capacity, it looks down upon gold and silver with the greatest disdain, considering them as the most immaterial and useless forms of capital. But as soon as it treats of the banking system, everything is reversed, and gold and silver become capital par excellence, for whose preservation every other form of capital and labor is to be sacrificed. But how are gold and silver distinguished from other forms of wealth? Not by the magnitude of their value, for this is determined by the quantity of labor materialized in them; but by the fact that they represent independent incarnations, expressions of the social character of wealth. This social existence assumes the aspect of a world beyond, of a thing, matter, commodity, by the side of and outside of the real elements of social wealth. So long as production is in a state of flux, this is forgotten. Credit, likewise, in its capacity as a social form of wealth, crowds money out and usurps its place. It is the faith in the social character of production which gives to the money-form of products the aspect of something disappearing and ideal. But as soon as credit is shaken—and this phase always appears of necessity in the cycles of modern industry—all the real wealth is to be actually and suddenly transformed into money, into gold and silver, a crazy demand, which, however, necessarily grows out of the system itself. And all the gold and silver which is supposed to satisfy these enormous demands, amounts to a few millions in the cellars of the banks!" (Karl Marx, Capital, Volume III)

It is not the money question, but the question of the entire capitalist production with everything implied by it, that interests the working people. And the general effect of this system upon the working class can be summarized in the one phrase: "progressive proletarianization." Capital is not primarily prevented from developing by the demands of the working class. It is prevented from ruling the world forever and holding down the working people for all eternity by its own immanent laws. It develops through contradictions. It cannot get away from them, because it is itself the greatest contradiction. It exists only in them and through them, and must finally fall through them. The antagonism between exploiters and exploited becomes more and more intense. It is transferred from the economic to the political field. Organized by the requirements of capitalist production itself, the proletariat adapts its economic organizations to the form of modern centralized industries, transforms its craft unions into industrial unions, unites its economic and political organizations in a well-planned division of labor, conquers the political power, and enables its economic organizations to take hold of the great sources of production and distribution in the interest of the working class, which remains the only essential class in society.

As soon as the working class controls the nation economically and politically, it inaugurates a system of collective production, in which the producers control their means of life, determine their own share in the cooperatively produced articles, and remove all obstacles to a full human development. Capitalism leaves the field to socialism.

Chapter 20   Closing Remarks

We have followed labor and capital through their long journey from primitive times to the present day. We have seen that human labor-power was the starting point, the mother and nurse, of capital, that capital grew and assumed many different forms, by which, in its turn, it determined the conditions under which human labor-power should be applied. We have seen that the existence, perpetuation and maintenance of capital have always rested, and still rest, upon the unpaid products of labor and the increasing productivity of labor.

The productive power of human labor has been, and still is, the impelling principle of social progress. Only by a distortion of historical facts and a disdain of palpable truths has the fiction of the benevolent role of capital arisen and maintained itself. But in proportion as capital approaches once more the critical stage where production reaches the end of its possibilities under the prevailing system of class rule, which precludes the possibility of any rescue from the rising tide of the proletarian revolution by interference from outside, the actual state of affairs claims recognition, and human labor once again, and for the last time, asserts its historical rights against a ruling class.

For thousands of years the ruling classes, the creatures of uncontrolled social laws, have ridden upon the backs of the producing classes. For thousands of years the rulers have driven the laboring classes and added to the natural spurs of human effort, to hunger and love, the lash and the whip.

We do not curse them for their cruelty, their greed, their disregard of human feeling, their prodigality of human lives. We know that the primal and unbridled forces of history molded them into masters with overbearing natures, and that the struggle for survival with its inexorable power lashed them forward as it did our class.

We know that the ruling classes have done much to increase the productivity of human labor. We realize that science and art have received much encouragement, if not inspiration, from them. But we do not close our eyes to the fact that the ruling classes produced all the progressive effects of their respective periods because they themselves had to have them. They wanted them, not for the purpose of benefiting "humanity," but of maintaining and enhancing their own position, and whatever they wanted they had to want, because the historical forces behind them compelled them to want just those things.

If we do not blame them for their faults, neither do we praise them for their virtues. Natural and social conditions made them and compelled them to be what they were and are.

But we, too, are the products of natural and social development. We, too, act and think as we must. And we feel as we must.

And we cannot feel, or think, or act in any other way than a revolutionary one. We see that the clash between the deeds and words of our masters is at bottom but the clash between their social interests and ours. Behind their inconsistencies lurk the natural and social forces, which they have tried in vain to fathom and control, but which we shall fathom and control by the very development which takes the ground from under the feet of the masters.

Calmly and coolly we proclaim the doom of the capitalist system and of the capitalist class. Firmly and unflinchingly we herald the coming of the co-operative commonwealth of economically equal workers. Our voice is the conscious voice of history itself.

Let the masters take heed and prepare! Let them stop the wheels of history if they can!